TEACHER'S PET PUBLICATIONS

PUZZLE PACK for
The Devil's Arithmetic

based on the book by
Jane Yolen

Written by
William T. Collins

© 2005 Teacher's Pet Publications
All Rights Reserved

The materials in this packet are copyrighted
by Teacher's Pet Publications, Inc.

These pages may be duplicated by the purchaser
for use in the purchaser's own classroom.

Copying any of these materials and distributing them
for any other purpose is a violation of the copyright laws.

© 2005 Teacher's Pet Publications, Inc.
www.tpet.com

INTRODUCTION
If you already own the LitPlan for this title, this Puzzle Pack will refresh your Unit Resource Materials and Vocabulary Resource Materials sections plus give you additional materials you can substitute into the tests. If you do not already have a complete LitPlan, these pages will give you some supplemental materials to use with your own plan. There are two main groups of materials: one set for unit words (such as characters' names, symbols, places, etc.) and one set for vocabulary words associated with the book.

WORD LIST
There is a word list for both the unit words and the vocabulary words. These lists show you which words are being used in the materials and the clues or definitions being used for those words. You may want to give students a word list with clues/definitions to help them, or you may want students to only have a word list (without clues/definitions) if you want them to work a little harder. Both are available for duplication. The word lists can also be your "calling key" for the bingo games.

FILL IN THE BLANK AND MATCHING
There are 4 each of the fill in the blank and matching worksheets for both the unit and vocabulary words. These pages can be used either as extra worksheets for students or as objective parts of a unit test. They can be done individually if students need extra help or as a whole class activity to review the material covered.

MAGIC SQUARES
The magic squares not only reinforce the material covered but also work on reasoning and math skills. Many teachers have told us that their students really enjoy doing these!

WORD SEARCH PUZZLES
The word search words go in all directions, as indicated on your answer keys. Two of the word search puzzles have the clues listed rather than the words. This makes the puzzle a little more difficult, but it reinforces the material better. Two word search puzzles have words only for students who find the clue puzzles too difficult.

CROSSWORD PUZZLES
Both unit and vocabulary word sections have 4 crossword puzzles.

BINGO CARDS
There are 32 individual bingo cards for the unit words and 32 individual bingo cards for the vocabulary words. You can use your word list as a "call list," calling the words at random and marking them off of your list as you go, or you could use the flash cards by cutting them apart and drawing the words at random from a hat (or box or whatever). To make a better review, you might ask for the definition and spelling of each word as you call it out–or you could call out the definitions and have students tell you the words they need to look for on the puzzle.

JUGGLE LETTERS
The vocabulary juggle letter game is intended to help students learn the spellings of the words. One sheet has the definitions listed on it as an extra help for students who need it or to reinforce the definitions if you choose to do so.

FLASH CARDS
We've included a set of vocabulary flash cards you can duplicate, cut, and fold for your students. Some teachers make a few sets for general use by the class; others make a set for each student. Some teachers duplicate them for each student and have the students cut & fold their own. You can cut out just the words and put them in a hat, have each student pick out one word and write the definition and a sentence for that word. Students then swap words and papers, with the next student adding a sentence of his own under the last one. You can have students swap as many times as you like. Each time the student will read the sentences written prior to his own and then add a sentence. You can cut out the words and definitions separately and play "I Have; Who Has?" Each student in the room draws a word and definition. The first student says, "I have (the name of the word). Who has the definition?" The student with the definition reads it then says, "I have (the name of the vocabulary word she has). Who has the definition?" The round continues until all words and definitions have been given.

Devil's Arithmetic Word List

No.	Word	Clue/Definition
1.	AARON	Called Ron-ron by his big sister Hannah
2.	AFIKOMAN	Matzoh wrapped in blue cloth and hidden
3.	ARITHMETIC	One plus one; each day alive
4.	BABUSHKA	Rivka's kerchief
5.	BASKET	Where Aaron hid the afikoman: clothes ___
6.	BORUCH	Fayge's rabbi father: Reb ___
7.	BREUR	Nazi camp commandant
8.	BRONX	Grandpa Will and Grandma Belle's residence
9.	BURNED	Tatooing pen did this to arm flesh
10.	CANOPY	Fayge and Shmuel were to married under one
11.	CAULDRONS	Huge soup kettles
12.	CHANUKAH	Eight day Jewish festival held in December
13.	CHOSEN	Those taken to the fire
14.	CLUCKING	Warning sound to children to hide
15.	COLD	Showers were ice ___
16.	EASTER	Christian holiday celebrated by Rosemary
17.	ELIJAH	Apartment door opened to welcome him
18.	EVA	Chaya's friend Rivka: Aunt ___
19.	FAYGE	Shmuel's fiance
20.	FINAL	Hitler's plan to rid the world of Jews: ___ solution
21.	FOUR	Number of days spent in the cattle cars
22.	GITL	Chaya's aunt
23.	HAGGADAH	Jewish guide book
24.	HANNAH	Time travels to Polish village in 1940's
25.	HEALTHY	Made to work hard at the camp
26.	HOLOCAUST	Mass destruction of European Jews
27.	INK	Used by a young Hannah to imitate her grandfather: blue ___
28.	KOMMANDOS	Jews made to carry the corpses
29.	KOSHER	Permitted according to Jewish law
30.	LILLITH	Gas ovens: ___'s Cave
31.	LUBLIN	Chaya's home village before joining Gitl
32.	MALACH	Angel of Death: ___ Ha-mavis
33.	MIDDEN	Garbage pile where children hid
34.	MUSSELMEN	Those who give up the fight
35.	ORGANIZE	Steal
36.	PASSOVER	Annual Jewish feast
37.	PROCESSED	Cremated
38.	QUESTIONS	Read by Aaron out of the Haggadah for the Seder: four ___
39.	RESETTLEMENT	Removing Jews to the concentration camps
40.	ROCHELLE	Hannah Stern's hometown: New ___
41.	SCHNELL	Yelled constantly to the Jews at the camp
42.	SEDER	Means order
43.	SHMUEL	Chaya's uncle who fails to escape camp
44.	SHORN	Done to Jews' hair
45.	SKY	God's canopy
46.	SWALLOWS	Sang around the smokestack
47.	TATTOO	Blue numbers burnt into flesh
48.	TWO	Number of villagers to survive camp
49.	VIOSK	Fayge's Polish village
50.	WILL	Kommando Wolfe as a boy: Grandpa ___
51.	WINE	Made Hannah's head hurt after she drank it

Copyrighted

Devil's Arithmetic Word List Continued

No.	Word	Clue/Definition
52.	WITNESS	To remember and tell so it won't happen again: bear ___
53.	WOLFE	Carried Fayge to Lillith's Cave
54.	YARMULKES	Little hats worn by men during ceremony
55.	YIDDISH	Spoken and understood by Chaya Abramowicz
56.	YITZCHAK	Butcher who escaped camp
57.	YOLEN	Author
58.	ZUGANGI	Newcomers

Devil's Arithmetic Fill In The Blank 1

_____ 1. Removing Jews to the concentration camps

_____ 2. Matzoh wrapped in blue cloth and hidden

_____ 3. Yelled constantly to the Jews at the camp

_____ 4. Used by a young Hannah to imitate her grandfather: blue ____

_____ 5. Showers were ice ____

_____ 6. Done to Jews' hair

_____ 7. Tatooing pen did this to arm flesh

_____ 8. Time travels to Polish village in 1940's

_____ 9. Fayge and Shmuel were to married under one

_____ 10. Warning sound to children to hide

_____ 11. Fayge's Polish village

_____ 12. Newcomers

_____ 13. Read by Aaron out of the Haggadah for the Seder: four ____

_____ 14. Christian holiday celebrated by Rosemary

_____ 15. Those taken to the fire

_____ 16. Kommando Wolfe as a boy: Grandpa ____

_____ 17. Shmuel's fiance

_____ 18. Means order

_____ 19. Where Aaron hid the afikoman: clothes ____

_____ 20. Chaya's home village before joining Gitl

Devil's Arithmetic Fill In The Blank 1 Answer Key

RESETTLEMENT	1. Removing Jews to the concentration camps
AFIKOMAN	2. Matzoh wrapped in blue cloth and hidden
SCHNELL	3. Yelled constantly to the Jews at the camp
INK	4. Used by a young Hannah to imitate her grandfather: blue ____
COLD	5. Showers were ice ____
SHORN	6. Done to Jews' hair
BURNED	7. Tatooing pen did this to arm flesh
HANNAH	8. Time travels to Polish village in 1940's
CANOPY	9. Fayge and Shmuel were to married under one
CLUCKING	10. Warning sound to children to hide
VIOSK	11. Fayge's Polish village
ZUGANGI	12. Newcomers
QUESTIONS	13. Read by Aaron out of the Haggadah for the Seder: four ____
EASTER	14. Christian holiday celebrated by Rosemary
CHOSEN	15. Those taken to the fire
WILL	16. Kommando Wolfe as a boy: Grandpa ___
FAYGE	17. Shmuel's fiance
SEDER	18. Means order
BASKET	19. Where Aaron hid the afikoman: clothes ___
LUBLIN	20. Chaya's home village before joining Gitl

Devil's Arithmetic Fill In The Blank 2

_____ 1. Hannah Stern's hometown: New ___

_____ 2. Done to Jews' hair

_____ 3. Carried Fayge to Lillith's Cave

_____ 4. Sang around the smokestack

_____ 5. Chaya's uncle who fails to escape camp

_____ 6. Gas ovens: ____'s Cave

_____ 7. Called Ron-ron by his big sister Hannah

_____ 8. Number of days spent in the cattle cars

_____ 9. Cremated

_____ 10. Blue numbers burnt into flesh

_____ 11. Mass destruction of European Jews

_____ 12. Removing Jews to the concentration camps

_____ 13. Jews made to carry the corpses

_____ 14. Where Aaron hid the afikoman: clothes ___

_____ 15. Butcher who escaped camp

_____ 16. Yelled constantly to the Jews at the camp

_____ 17. Eight day Jewish festival held in December

_____ 18. Rivka's kerchief

_____ 19. One plus one; each day alive

_____ 20. Kommando Wolfe as a boy: Grandpa ___

Devil's Arithmetic Fill In The Blank 2 Answer Key

ROCHELLE	1. Hannah Stern's hometown: New ___
SHORN	2. Done to Jews' hair
WOLFE	3. Carried Fayge to Lillith's Cave
SWALLOWS	4. Sang around the smokestack
SHMUEL	5. Chaya's uncle who fails to escape camp
LILLITH	6. Gas ovens: ____'s Cave
AARON	7. Called Ron-ron by his big sister Hannah
FOUR	8. Number of days spent in the cattle cars
PROCESSED	9. Cremated
TATTOO	10. Blue numbers burnt into flesh
HOLOCAUST	11. Mass destruction of European Jews
RESETTLEMENT	12. Removing Jews to the concentration camps
KOMMANDOS	13. Jews made to carry the corpses
BASKET	14. Where Aaron hid the afikoman: clothes ___
YITZCHAK	15. Butcher who escaped camp
SCHNELL	16. Yelled constantly to the Jews at the camp
CHANUKAH	17. Eight day Jewish festival held in December
BABUSHKA	18. Rivka's kerchief
ARITHMETIC	19. One plus one; each day alive
WILL	20. Kommando Wolfe as a boy: Grandpa ___

Devil's Arithmetic Fill In The Blank 3

_____ 1. Called Ron-ron by his big sister Hannah

_____ 2. Mass destruction of European Jews

_____ 3. Steal

_____ 4. Where Aaron hid the afikoman: clothes ___

_____ 5. Done to Jews' hair

_____ 6. Rivka's kerchief

_____ 7. Read by Aaron out of the Haggadah for the Seder: four ____

_____ 8. Made to work hard at the camp

_____ 9. Shmuel's fiance

_____ 10. Spoken and understood by Chaya Abramowicz

_____ 11. Made Hannah's head hurt after she drank it

_____ 12. Blue numbers burnt into flesh

_____ 13. Author

_____ 14. Those who give up the fight

_____ 15. Warning sound to children to hide

_____ 16. Fayge and Shmuel were to married under one

_____ 17. Huge soup kettles

_____ 18. Kommando Wolfe as a boy: Grandpa ___

_____ 19. Cremated

_____ 20. Tatooing pen did this to arm flesh

Devil's Arithmetic Fill In The Blank 3 Answer Key

AARON	1. Called Ron-ron by his big sister Hannah
HOLOCAUST	2. Mass destruction of European Jews
ORGANIZE	3. Steal
BASKET	4. Where Aaron hid the afikoman: clothes ___
SHORN	5. Done to Jews' hair
BABUSHKA	6. Rivka's kerchief
QUESTIONS	7. Read by Aaron out of the Haggadah for the Seder: four ____
HEALTHY	8. Made to work hard at the camp
FAYGE	9. Shmuel's fiance
YIDDISH	10. Spoken and understood by Chaya Abramowicz
WINE	11. Made Hannah's head hurt after she drank it
TATTOO	12. Blue numbers burnt into flesh
YOLEN	13. Author
MUSSELMEN	14. Those who give up the fight
CLUCKING	15. Warning sound to children to hide
CANOPY	16. Fayge and Shmuel were to married under one
CAULDRONS	17. Huge soup kettles
WILL	18. Kommando Wolfe as a boy: Grandpa ___
PROCESSED	19. Cremated
BURNED	20. Tatooing pen did this to arm flesh

Devil's Arithmetic Fill In The Blank 4

_____   1. Little hats worn by men during ceremony
_____   2. Hannah Stern's hometown: New ___
_____   3. Nazi camp commandant
_____   4. Tatooing pen did this to arm flesh
_____   5. Rivka's kerchief
_____   6. Kommando Wolfe as a boy: Grandpa ___
_____   7. One plus one; each day alive
_____   8. Cremated
_____   9. Chaya's aunt
_____   10. Made to work hard at the camp
_____   11. Steal
_____   12. Matzoh wrapped in blue cloth and hidden
_____   13. Eight day Jewish festival held in December
_____   14. Spoken and understood by Chaya Abramowicz
_____   15. Chaya's friend Rivka: Aunt ___
_____   16. To remember and tell so it won't happen again: bear ___
_____   17. Means order
_____   18. Where Aaron hid the afikoman: clothes ___
_____   19. Chaya's home village before joining Gitl
_____   20. Permitted according to Jewish law

Devil's Arithmetic Fill In The Blank 4 Answer Key

YARMULKES	1. Little hats worn by men during ceremony
ROCHELLE	2. Hannah Stern's hometown: New ___
BREUR	3. Nazi camp commandant
BURNED	4. Tatooing pen did this to arm flesh
BABUSHKA	5. Rivka's kerchief
WILL	6. Kommando Wolfe as a boy: Grandpa ___
ARITHMETIC	7. One plus one; each day alive
PROCESSED	8. Cremated
GITL	9. Chaya's aunt
HEALTHY	10. Made to work hard at the camp
ORGANIZE	11. Steal
AFIKOMAN	12. Matzoh wrapped in blue cloth and hidden
CHANUKAH	13. Eight day Jewish festival held in December
YIDDISH	14. Spoken and understood by Chaya Abramowicz
EVA	15. Chaya's friend Rivka: Aunt ___
WITNESS	16. To remember and tell so it won't happen again: bear ___
SEDER	17. Means order
BASKET	18. Where Aaron hid the afikoman: clothes ___
LUBLIN	19. Chaya's home village before joining Gitl
KOSHER	20. Permitted according to Jewish law

Devil's Arithmetic Matching 1

___ 1. KOSHER   A. Done to Jews' hair
___ 2. FAYGE   B. Hannah Stern's hometown: New ___
___ 3. ZUGANGI   C. Garbage pile where children hid
___ 4. SHMUEL   D. One plus one; each day alive
___ 5. SHORN   E. Warning sound to children to hide
___ 6. ELIJAH   F. Those taken to the fire
___ 7. BRONX   G. Chaya's home village before joining Gitl
___ 8. FOUR   H. Chaya's uncle who fails to escape camp
___ 9. CLUCKING   I. Fayge and Shmuel were to married under one
___10. ROCHELLE   J. Newcomers
___11. TATTOO   K. Tatooing pen did this to arm flesh
___12. BURNED   L. Shmuel's fiance
___13. ARITHMETIC   M. Rivka's kerchief
___14. CHOSEN   N. Jewish guide book
___15. WITNESS   O. Grandpa Will and Grandma Belle's residence
___16. BORUCH   P. Apartment door opened to welcome him
___17. CHANUKAH   Q. Blue numbers burnt into flesh
___18. CANOPY   R. Fayge's rabbi father: Reb ___
___19. VIOSK   S. To remember and tell so it won't happen again: bear ___
___20. BABUSHKA   T. Permitted according to Jewish law
___21. YOLEN   U. Author
___22. LUBLIN   V. Eight day Jewish festival held in December
___23. HAGGADAH   W. Used by a young Hannah to imitate her grandfather: blue ___
___24. MIDDEN   X. Fayge's Polish village
___25. INK   Y. Number of days spent in the cattle cars

Devil's Arithmetic Matching 1 Answer Key

T - 1.	KOSHER	A. Done to Jews' hair
L - 2.	FAYGE	B. Hannah Stern's hometown: New ___
J - 3.	ZUGANGI	C. Garbage pile where children hid
H - 4.	SHMUEL	D. One plus one; each day alive
A - 5.	SHORN	E. Warning sound to children to hide
P - 6.	ELIJAH	F. Those taken to the fire
O - 7.	BRONX	G. Chaya's home village before joining Gitl
Y - 8.	FOUR	H. Chaya's uncle who fails to escape camp
E - 9.	CLUCKING	I. Fayge and Shmuel were to married under one
B - 10.	ROCHELLE	J. Newcomers
Q - 11.	TATTOO	K. Tatooing pen did this to arm flesh
K - 12.	BURNED	L. Shmuel's fiance
D - 13.	ARITHMETIC	M. Rivka's kerchief
F - 14.	CHOSEN	N. Jewish guide book
S - 15.	WITNESS	O. Grandpa Will and Grandma Belle's residence
R - 16.	BORUCH	P. Apartment door opened to welcome him
V - 17.	CHANUKAH	Q. Blue numbers burnt into flesh
I - 18.	CANOPY	R. Fayge's rabbi father: Reb ___
X - 19.	VIOSK	S. To remember and tell so it won't happen again: bear ___
M - 20.	BABUSHKA	T. Permitted according to Jewish law
U - 21.	YOLEN	U. Author
G - 22.	LUBLIN	V. Eight day Jewish festival held in December
N - 23.	HAGGADAH	W. Used by a young Hannah to imitate her grandfather: blue ___
C - 24.	MIDDEN	X. Fayge's Polish village
W - 25.	INK	Y. Number of days spent in the cattle cars

Devil's Arithmetic Matching 2

___ 1. SEDER
___ 2. SHMUEL
___ 3. SCHNELL
___ 4. KOSHER
___ 5. HEALTHY
___ 6. KOMMANDOS
___ 7. FOUR
___ 8. MUSSELMEN
___ 9. YARMULKES
___ 10. FINAL
___ 11. ARITHMETIC
___ 12. RESETTLEMENT
___ 13. BURNED
___ 14. HOLOCAUST
___ 15. BORUCH
___ 16. GITL
___ 17. INK
___ 18. MALACH
___ 19. WITNESS
___ 20. YIDDISH
___ 21. BASKET
___ 22. CLUCKING
___ 23. WOLFE
___ 24. CHOSEN
___ 25. SHORN

A. Spoken and understood by Chaya Abramowicz
B. Hitler's plan to rid the world of Jews: ____ solution
C. Chaya's aunt
D. Fayge's rabbi father: Reb ___
E. Chaya's uncle who fails to escape camp
F. Those taken to the fire
G. Number of days spent in the cattle cars
H. Where Aaron hid the afikoman: clothes ___
I. Made to work hard at the camp
J. Jews made to carry the corpses
K. Those who give up the fight
L. Means order
M. Yelled constantly to the Jews at the camp
N. Mass destruction of European Jews
O. To remember and tell so it won't happen again: bear ___
P. Permitted according to Jewish law
Q. One plus one; each day alive
R. Warning sound to children to hide
S. Angel of Death: ____ Ha-mavis
T. Used by a young Hannah to imitate her grandfather: blue ___
U. Little hats worn by men during ceremony
V. Carried Fayge to Lillith's Cave
W. Tatooing pen did this to arm flesh
X. Done to Jews' hair
Y. Removing Jews to the concentration camps

Devil's Arithmetic Matching 2 Answer Key

L - 1. SEDER		A. Spoken and understood by Chaya Abramowicz
E - 2. SHMUEL		B. Hitler's plan to rid the world of Jews: ____ solution
M - 3. SCHNELL		C. Chaya's aunt
P - 4. KOSHER		D. Fayge's rabbi father: Reb ___
I - 5. HEALTHY		E. Chaya's uncle who fails to escape camp
J - 6. KOMMANDOS		F. Those taken to the fire
G - 7. FOUR		G. Number of days spent in the cattle cars
K - 8. MUSSELMEN		H. Where Aaron hid the afikoman: clothes ___
U - 9. YARMULKES		I. Made to work hard at the camp
B - 10. FINAL		J. Jews made to carry the corpses
Q - 11. ARITHMETIC		K. Those who give up the fight
Y - 12. RESETTLEMENT		L. Means order
W - 13. BURNED		M. Yelled constantly to the Jews at the camp
N - 14. HOLOCAUST		N. Mass destruction of European Jews
D - 15. BORUCH		O. To remember and tell so it won't happen again: bear ___
C - 16. GITL		P. Permitted according to Jewish law
T - 17. INK		Q. One plus one; each day alive
S - 18. MALACH		R. Warning sound to children to hide
O - 19. WITNESS		S. Angel of Death: ____ Ha-mavis
A - 20. YIDDISH		T. Used by a young Hannah to imitate her grandfather: blue ___
H - 21. BASKET		U. Little hats worn by men during ceremony
R - 22. CLUCKING		V. Carried Fayge to Lillith's Cave
V - 23. WOLFE		W. Tatooing pen did this to arm flesh
F - 24. CHOSEN		X. Done to Jews' hair
X - 25. SHORN		Y. Removing Jews to the concentration camps

Copyrighted

Devil's Arithmetic Matching 3

___ 1. SHMUEL   A. Chaya's uncle who fails to escape camp
___ 2. INK   B. Used by a young Hannah to imitate her grandfather: blue ___
___ 3. CLUCKING   C. Fayge's Polish village
___ 4. HANNAH   D. Spoken and understood by Chaya Abramowicz
___ 5. SEDER   E. Yelled constantly to the Jews at the camp
___ 6. SCHNELL   F. Permitted according to Jewish law
___ 7. MIDDEN   G. Made Hannah's head hurt after she drank it
___ 8. YOLEN   H. Garbage pile where children hid
___ 9. VIOSK   I. Kommando Wolfe as a boy: Grandpa ___
___ 10. GITL   J. Huge soup kettles
___ 11. YIDDISH   K. Number of days spent in the cattle cars
___ 12. TATTOO   L. Done to Jews' hair
___ 13. KOSHER   M. Apartment door opened to welcome him
___ 14. WILL   N. Blue numbers burnt into flesh
___ 15. ELIJAH   O. Made to work hard at the camp
___ 16. HEALTHY   P. Those who give up the fight
___ 17. MALACH   Q. Means order
___ 18. KOMMANDOS   R. Gas ovens: ____'s Cave
___ 19. FOUR   S. Jews made to carry the corpses
___ 20. LILLITH   T. Chaya's aunt
___ 21. WOLFE   U. Author
___ 22. WINE   V. Angel of Death: ____ Ha-mavis
___ 23. CAULDRONS   W. Carried Fayge to Lillith's Cave
___ 24. SHORN   X. Time travels to Polish village in 1940's
___ 25. MUSSELMEN   Y. Warning sound to children to hide

Devil's Arithmetic Matching 3 Answer Key

A - 1. SHMUEL	A.	Chaya's uncle who fails to escape camp
B - 2. INK	B.	Used by a young Hannah to imitate her grandfather: blue ___
Y - 3. CLUCKING	C.	Fayge's Polish village
X - 4. HANNAH	D.	Spoken and understood by Chaya Abramowicz
Q - 5. SEDER	E.	Yelled constantly to the Jews at the camp
E - 6. SCHNELL	F.	Permitted according to Jewish law
H - 7. MIDDEN	G.	Made Hannah's head hurt after she drank it
U - 8. YOLEN	H.	Garbage pile where children hid
C - 9. VIOSK	I.	Kommando Wolfe as a boy: Grandpa ___
T - 10. GITL	J.	Huge soup kettles
D - 11. YIDDISH	K.	Number of days spent in the cattle cars
N - 12. TATTOO	L.	Done to Jews' hair
F - 13. KOSHER	M.	Apartment door opened to welcome him
I - 14. WILL	N.	Blue numbers burnt into flesh
M - 15. ELIJAH	O.	Made to work hard at the camp
O - 16. HEALTHY	P.	Those who give up the fight
V - 17. MALACH	Q.	Means order
S - 18. KOMMANDOS	R.	Gas ovens: ___'s Cave
K - 19. FOUR	S.	Jews made to carry the corpses
R - 20. LILLITH	T.	Chaya's aunt
W - 21. WOLFE	U.	Author
G - 22. WINE	V.	Angel of Death: ___ Ha-mavis
J - 23. CAULDRONS	W.	Carried Fayge to Lillith's Cave
L - 24. SHORN	X.	Time travels to Polish village in 1940's
P - 25. MUSSELMEN	Y.	Warning sound to children to hide

Devil's Arithmetic Matching 4

___ 1. LUBLIN
___ 2. SCHNELL
___ 3. EASTER
___ 4. HANNAH
___ 5. LILLITH
___ 6. SHMUEL
___ 7. BURNED
___ 8. SKY
___ 9. WITNESS
___ 10. KOSHER
___ 11. TWO
___ 12. HAGGADAH
___ 13. ORGANIZE
___ 14. ROCHELLE
___ 15. PASSOVER
___ 16. AARON
___ 17. BASKET
___ 18. YITZCHAK
___ 19. BREUR
___ 20. RESETTLEMENT
___ 21. FOUR
___ 22. MIDDEN
___ 23. INK
___ 24. HOLOCAUST
___ 25. CAULDRONS

A. Yelled constantly to the Jews at the camp
B. Called Ron-ron by his big sister Hannah
C. Gas ovens: ____'s Cave
D. Chaya's home village before joining Gitl
E. Tatooing pen did this to arm flesh
F. Removing Jews to the concentration camps
G. Nazi camp commandant
H. Used by a young Hannah to imitate her grandfather: blue ___
I. Hannah Stern's hometown: New ___
J. Huge soup kettles
K. Chaya's uncle who fails to escape camp
L. Where Aaron hid the afikoman: clothes ___
M. Time travels to Polish village in 1940's
N. Butcher who escaped camp
O. God's canopy
P. Christian holiday celebrated by Rosemary
Q. Jewish guide book
R. Number of days spent in the cattle cars
S. Permitted according to Jewish law
T. Steal
U. To remember and tell so it won't happen again: bear ___
V. Annual Jewish feast
W. Garbage pile where children hid
X. Number of villagers to survive camp
Y. Mass destruction of European Jews

Devil's Arithmetic Matching 4 Answer Key

D - 1.	LUBLIN	A.	Yelled constantly to the Jews at the camp
A - 2.	SCHNELL	B.	Called Ron-ron by his big sister Hannah
P - 3.	EASTER	C.	Gas ovens: ____'s Cave
M - 4.	HANNAH	D.	Chaya's home village before joining Gitl
C - 5.	LILLITH	E.	Tatooing pen did this to arm flesh
K - 6.	SHMUEL	F.	Removing Jews to the concentration camps
E - 7.	BURNED	G.	Nazi camp commandant
O - 8.	SKY	H.	Used by a young Hannah to imitate her grandfather: blue ___
U - 9.	WITNESS	I.	Hannah Stern's hometown: New ___
S - 10.	KOSHER	J.	Huge soup kettles
X - 11.	TWO	K.	Chaya's uncle who fails to escape camp
Q - 12.	HAGGADAH	L.	Where Aaron hid the afikoman: clothes ___
T - 13.	ORGANIZE	M.	Time travels to Polish village in 1940's
I - 14.	ROCHELLE	N.	Butcher who escaped camp
V - 15.	PASSOVER	O.	God's canopy
B - 16.	AARON	P.	Christian holiday celebrated by Rosemary
L - 17.	BASKET	Q.	Jewish guide book
N - 18.	YITZCHAK	R.	Number of days spent in the cattle cars
G - 19.	BREUR	S.	Permitted according to Jewish law
F - 20.	RESETTLEMENT	T.	Steal
R - 21.	FOUR	U.	To remember and tell so it won't happen again: bear ___
W - 22.	MIDDEN	V.	Annual Jewish feast
H - 23.	INK	W.	Garbage pile where children hid
Y - 24.	HOLOCAUST	X.	Number of villagers to survive camp
J - 25.	CAULDRONS	Y.	Mass destruction of European Jews

Devil's Arithmetic Magic Squares 1

Match the definition with the vocabulary word. Put your answers in the magic squares below. When your answers are correct, all columns and rows will add to the same number.

A. BORUCH
B. SCHNELL
C. RESETTLEMENT
D. SHORN
E. AFIKOMAN
F. LILLITH
G. CHANUKAH
H. TATTOO
I. EVA
J. BREUR
K. GITL
L. INK
M. CAULDRONS
N. FINAL
O. MALACH
P. ELIJAH

1. Removing Jews to the concentration camps
2. Nazi camp commandant
3. Gas ovens: ____'s Cave
4. Angel of Death: ____ Ha-mavis
5. Apartment door opened to welcome him
6. Matzoh wrapped in blue cloth and hidden
7. Chaya's friend Rivka: Aunt ____
8. Done to Jews' hair
9. Huge soup kettles
10. Blue numbers burnt into flesh
11. Used by a young Hannah to imitate her grandfather: blue ____
12. Fayge's rabbi father: Reb ____
13. Yelled constantly to the Jews at the camp
14. Chaya's aunt
15. Eight day Jewish festival held in December
16. Hitler's plan to rid the world of Jews: ____ solution

A=	B=	C=	D=
E=	F=	G=	H=
I=	J=	K=	L=
M=	N=	O=	P=

Devil's Arithmetic Magic Squares 1 Answer Key

Match the definition with the vocabulary word. Put your answers in the magic squares below. When your answers are correct, all columns and rows will add to the same number.

A. BORUCH
B. SCHNELL
C. RESETTLEMENT
D. SHORN
E. AFIKOMAN
F. LILLITH
G. CHANUKAH
H. TATTOO
I. EVA
J. BREUR
K. GITL
L. INK
M. CAULDRONS
N. FINAL
O. MALACH
P. ELIJAH

1. Removing Jews to the concentration camps
2. Nazi camp commandant
3. Gas ovens: ____'s Cave
4. Angel of Death: ____ Ha-mavis
5. Apartment door opened to welcome him
6. Matzoh wrapped in blue cloth and hidden
7. Chaya's friend Rivka: Aunt ___
8. Done to Jews' hair
9. Huge soup kettles
10. Blue numbers burnt into flesh
11. Used by a young Hannah to imitate her grandfather: blue ___
12. Fayge's rabbi father: Reb ___
13. Yelled constantly to the Jews at the camp
14. Chaya's aunt
15. Eight day Jewish festival held in December
16. Hitler's plan to rid the world of Jews: ____ solution

A=12	B=13	C=1	D=8
E=6	F=3	G=15	H=10
I=7	J=2	K=14	L=11
M=9	N=16	O=4	P=5

Devil's Arithmetic Magic Squares 2

Match the definition with the vocabulary word. Put your answers in the magic squares below. When your answers are correct, all columns and rows will add to the same number.

A. HEALTHY
B. WILL
C. VIOSK
D. BASKET
E. FINAL
F. CLUCKING
G. ARITHMETIC
H. AFIKOMAN
I. KOSHER
J. GITL
K. BRONX
L. KOMMANDOS
M. SKY
N. BABUSHKA
O. EASTER
P. ROCHELLE

1. Christian holiday celebrated by Rosemary
2. Where Aaron hid the afikoman: clothes ___
3. Chaya's aunt
4. Hitler's plan to rid the world of Jews: ____ solution
5. Permitted according to Jewish law
6. Warning sound to children to hide
7. Hannah Stern's hometown: New ___
8. Fayge's Polish village
9. Matzoh wrapped in blue cloth and hidden
10. Grandpa Will and Grandma Belle's residence
11. Made to work hard at the camp
12. Rivka's kerchief
13. Kommando Wolfe as a boy: Grandpa ___
14. God's canopy
15. One plus one; each day alive
16. Jews made to carry the corpses

A=	B=	C=	D=
E=	F=	G=	H=
I=	J=	K=	L=
M=	N=	O=	P=

Devil's Arithmetic Magic Squares 2 Answer Key

Match the definition with the vocabulary word. Put your answers in the magic squares below. When your answers are correct, all columns and rows will add to the same number.

A. HEALTHY
B. WILL
C. VIOSK
D. BASKET
E. FINAL
F. CLUCKING
G. ARITHMETIC
H. AFIKOMAN
I. KOSHER
J. GITL
K. BRONX
L. KOMMANDOS
M. SKY
N. BABUSHKA
O. EASTER
P. ROCHELLE

1. Christian holiday celebrated by Rosemary
2. Where Aaron hid the afikoman: clothes ___
3. Chaya's aunt
4. Hitler's plan to rid the world of Jews: ____ solution
5. Permitted according to Jewish law
6. Warning sound to children to hide
7. Hannah Stern's hometown: New ___
8. Fayge's Polish village
9. Matzoh wrapped in blue cloth and hidden
10. Grandpa Will and Grandma Belle's residence
11. Made to work hard at the camp
12. Rivka's kerchief
13. Kommando Wolfe as a boy: Grandpa ___
14. God's canopy
15. One plus one; each day alive
16. Jews made to carry the corpses

A=11	B=13	C=8	D=2
E=4	F=6	G=15	H=9
I=5	J=3	K=10	L=16
M=14	N=12	O=1	P=7

Devil's Arithmetic Magic Squares 3

Match the definition with the vocabulary word. Put your answers in the magic squares below. When your answers are correct, all columns and rows will add to the same number.

A. CANOPY
B. YOLEN
C. ROCHELLE
D. WILL
E. WOLFE
F. BASKET
G. GITL
H. KOSHER
I. YARMULKES
J. EASTER
K. YIDDISH
L. VIOSK
M. CHANUKAH
N. INK
O. AFIKOMAN
P. KOMMANDOS

1. Matzoh wrapped in blue cloth and hidden
2. Christian holiday celebrated by Rosemary
3. Permitted according to Jewish law
4. Fayge and Shmuel were to married under one
5. Kommando Wolfe as a boy: Grandpa ___
6. Carried Fayge to Lillith's Cave
7. Spoken and understood by Chaya Abramowicz
8. Used by a young Hannah to imitate her grandfather: blue ___
9. Where Aaron hid the afikoman: clothes ___
10. Hannah Stern's hometown: New ___
11. Eight day Jewish festival held in December
12. Fayge's Polish village
13. Little hats worn by men during ceremony
14. Jews made to carry the corpses
15. Author
16. Chaya's aunt

A=	B=	C=	D=
E=	F=	G=	H=
I=	J=	K=	L=
M=	N=	O=	P=

Devil's Arithmetic Magic Squares 3 Answer Key

Match the definition with the vocabulary word. Put your answers in the magic squares below. When your answers are correct, all columns and rows will add to the same number.

A. CANOPY
B. YOLEN
C. ROCHELLE
D. WILL
E. WOLFE
F. BASKET
G. GITL
H. KOSHER
I. YARMULKES
J. EASTER
K. YIDDISH
L. VIOSK
M. CHANUKAH
N. INK
O. AFIKOMAN
P. KOMMANDOS

1. Matzoh wrapped in blue cloth and hidden
2. Christian holiday celebrated by Rosemary
3. Permitted according to Jewish law
4. Fayge and Shmuel were to married under one
5. Kommando Wolfe as a boy: Grandpa ___
6. Carried Fayge to Lillith's Cave
7. Spoken and understood by Chaya Abramowicz
8. Used by a young Hannah to imitate her grandfather: blue ___
9. Where Aaron hid the afikoman: clothes ___
10. Hannah Stern's hometown: New ___
11. Eight day Jewish festival held in December
12. Fayge's Polish village
13. Little hats worn by men during ceremony
14. Jews made to carry the corpses
15. Author
16. Chaya's aunt

A=4	B=15	C=10	D=5
E=6	F=9	G=16	H=3
I=13	J=2	K=7	L=12
M=11	N=8	O=1	P=14

Devil's Arithmetic Magic Squares 4

Match the definition with the vocabulary word. Put your answers in the magic squares below. When your answers are correct, all columns and rows will add to the same number.

A. WINE
B. FOUR
C. CHOSEN
D. ROCHELLE
E. MIDDEN
F. SHMUEL
G. BASKET
H. YOLEN
I. CLUCKING
J. COLD
K. SCHNELL
L. ELIJAH
M. MUSSELMEN
N. BABUSHKA
O. ZUGANGI
P. WILL

1. Author
2. Those who give up the fight
3. Number of days spent in the cattle cars
4. Yelled constantly to the Jews at the camp
5. Showers were ice ____
6. Those taken to the fire
7. Kommando Wolfe as a boy: Grandpa ____
8. Garbage pile where children hid
9. Newcomers
10. Chaya's uncle who fails to escape camp
11. Warning sound to children to hide
12. Hannah Stern's hometown: New ____
13. Made Hannah's head hurt after she drank it
14. Apartment door opened to welcome him
15. Where Aaron hid the afikoman: clothes ____
16. Rivka's kerchief

A=	B=	C=	D=
E=	F=	G=	H=
I=	J=	K=	L=
M=	N=	O=	P=

Devil's Arithmetic Magic Squares 4 Answer Key

Match the definition with the vocabulary word. Put your answers in the magic squares below. When your answers are correct, all columns and rows will add to the same number.

A. WINE
B. FOUR
C. CHOSEN
D. ROCHELLE
E. MIDDEN
F. SHMUEL
G. BASKET
H. YOLEN
I. CLUCKING
J. COLD
K. SCHNELL
L. ELIJAH
M. MUSSELMEN
N. BABUSHKA
O. ZUGANGI
P. WILL

1. Author
2. Those who give up the fight
3. Number of days spent in the cattle cars
4. Yelled constantly to the Jews at the camp
5. Showers were ice ____
6. Those taken to the fire
7. Kommando Wolfe as a boy: Grandpa ____
8. Garbage pile where children hid
9. Newcomers
10. Chaya's uncle who fails to escape camp
11. Warning sound to children to hide
12. Hannah Stern's hometown: New ____
13. Made Hannah's head hurt after she drank it
14. Apartment door opened to welcome him
15. Where Aaron hid the afikoman: clothes ____
16. Rivka's kerchief

A=13	B=3	C=6	D=12
E=8	F=10	G=15	H=1
I=11	J=5	K=4	L=14
M=2	N=16	O=9	P=7

Devil's Arithmetic Word Search 1

```
Z L T N E M E L T T E S E R R Y W L
U U C E N S T T E W Z G U E I I I B
G B V M V I K K M O Y E V D N C T L
A L I L G N S D Z A R O D E L S N R
N I O E I A E H F B S I L S G D E C
G N S S B N G Y P S S L N Q L H S G
I Y K S R P L M A H E H B O S H S J
Y R L U Z D N P M N T C C O E D K H
O Z B M L E U M H S M U K F E V A C
L Y T A L Q S C U N C R L Q O D K R
E K A A F P S A E O T O Y L A U O M
N O T R K W C N L R W B L G Y C R M
D M T O M O F A I D L I G T H H G Z
S M O N L U C M J L W A F E T A A D
H A O O M B L O A U H P L C L N N Y
O N H F A R R K H A H L H A A U I R
R D Y Y L O W I E C E O M N E K Z X
N O K L A N I F T S S X R O H A E C
F S V W C X Q A Z E B J W P N H H J
Z C V Z H H A N N A H B W Y H F B Y
```

Angel of Death: ____ Ha-mavis (6)
Annual Jewish feast (8)
Apartment door opened to welcome him (6)
Author (5)
Blue numbers burnt into flesh (6)
Called Ron-ron by his big sister Hannah (5)
Carried Fayge to Lillith's Cave (5)
Chaya's aunt (4)
Chaya's friend Rivka: Aunt ___ (3)
Chaya's home village before joining Gitl (6)
Chaya's uncle who fails to escape camp (6)
Done to Jews' hair (5)
Eight day Jewish festival held in December (8)
Fayge and Shmuel were to married under one (6)
Fayge's Polish village (5)
Fayge's rabbi father: Reb ___ (6)
God's canopy (3)
Grandpa Will and Grandma Belle's residence (5)
Hannah Stern's hometown: New ___ (8)
Hitler's plan to rid the world of Jews: ____ solution (5)
Huge soup kettles (9)
Jewish guide book (8)
Jews made to carry the corpses (9)
Kommando Wolfe as a boy: Grandpa ___ (4)
Little hats worn by men during ceremony (9)

Made Hannah's head hurt after she drank it (4)
Made to work hard at the camp (7)
Mass destruction of European Jews (9)
Matzoh wrapped in blue cloth and hidden (8)
Means order (5)
Nazi camp commandant (5)
Newcomers (7)
Number of days spent in the cattle cars (4)
Number of villagers to survive camp (3)
Permitted according to Jewish law (6)
Removing Jews to the concentration camps (12)
Shmuel's fiance (5)
Showers were ice ____ (4)
Spoken and understood by Chaya Abramowicz (7)
Steal (8)
Tatooing pen did this to arm flesh (6)
Those taken to the fire (6)
Those who give up the fight (9)
Time travels to Polish village in 1940's (6)
To remember and tell so it won't happen again: bear ___ (7)
Used by a young Hannah to imitate her grandfather: blue ___ (3)
Where Aaron hid the afikoman: clothes ___ (6)
Yelled constantly to the Jews at the camp (7)

Devil's Arithmetic Word Search 1 Answer Key

```
Z L T N E M E L T T E S E R R Y W
U U E T E W G U E I I I
G B V M I K K O Y E V D N T
A L I L G N S D A R O D E N R
N I O E I A E F B S I L S D E
G N S S B N S S L L H S
I K S R A H E H O S S
Y U P N T C C O E H
O B M L E U M H S U K F E V A
L Y T A C U N R L O D R
E K A A S A E O O L A U O
N O T R C N L R W B L G Y C R
M T O M O A I D I G H H G
S M O N L U M J L W A E T A
H A O O M B L O A U H L C L N
O N H A R K H A L H A A U I
R D Y L O I E C E O N E K Z
N O K L A N I F S S O H A E
S C X A E P Y
H H A N N A H
```

Angel of Death: ____ Ha-mavis (6)
Annual Jewish feast (8)
Apartment door opened to welcome him (6)
Author (5)
Blue numbers burnt into flesh (6)
Called Ron-ron by his big sister Hannah (5)
Carried Fayge to Lillith's Cave (5)
Chaya's aunt (4)
Chaya's friend Rivka: Aunt ____ (3)
Chaya's home village before joining Gitl (6)
Chaya's uncle who fails to escape camp (6)
Done to Jews' hair (5)
Eight day Jewish festival held in December (8)
Fayge and Shmuel were to married under one (6)
Fayge's Polish village (5)
Fayge's rabbi father: Reb ____ (6)
God's canopy (3)
Grandpa Will and Grandma Belle's residence (5)
Hannah Stern's hometown: New ____ (8)
Hitler's plan to rid the world of Jews: ____ solution (5)
Huge soup kettles (9)
Jewish guide book (8)
Jews made to carry the corpses (9)
Kommando Wolfe as a boy: Grandpa ____ (4)
Little hats worn by men during ceremony (9)

Made Hannah's head hurt after she drank it (4)
Made to work hard at the camp (7)
Mass destruction of European Jews (9)
Matzoh wrapped in blue cloth and hidden (8)
Means order (5)
Nazi camp commandant (5)
Newcomers (7)
Number of days spent in the cattle cars (4)
Number of villagers to survive camp (3)
Permitted according to Jewish law (6)
Removing Jews to the concentration camps (12)
Shmuel's fiance (5)
Showers were ice ____ (4)
Spoken and understood by Chaya Abramowicz (7)
Steal (8)
Tatooing pen did this to arm flesh (6)
Those taken to the fire (6)
Those who give up the fight (9)
Time travels to Polish village in 1940's (6)
To remember and tell so it won't happen again: bear ____ (7)
Used by a young Hannah to imitate her grandfather: blue ____ (3)
Where Aaron hid the afikoman: clothes ____ (6)
Yelled constantly to the Jews at the camp (7)

Devil's Arithmetic Word Search 2

```
V C M C Y W I L L D E S S E C O R P
H L H B A I H A J I L E S B T L B R
T U A O L N D Q M Y E D E A J K R Z
T C G R Z T O D B M L E N S P T O Y
M K G U F M G P I P L R T K E O K F
C I A C D S I S Y S E Z I E T V F R
B N D H Y H T L A E H O W T R S A M
Y G A D Y O L D J O C P A E E F Y D
Q C H W E R E K L S O T T K I I G Q
K O M M A N D O S Z R S L K H N E Q
P R G X R Q C S K H A U O A I A N J
A G K U R A N H Y E M M K L L L I Z
S A B R U O F E X R A U B P I C W C
S N X S E Q K R A N N U E K L H L F
O I T D R N V Y C A L D H L L O B D
V Z N X B X I N H H E C Q N I S G G
E E G K N M O C H F A O E Q T E M S
R J J O P R S D L L C L T T H N J T
L C R Q A T K O A T O D H A N N A H
R B V A C L W M Z Y B A B U S H K A
```

Angel of Death: ____ Ha-mavis (6)
Annual Jewish feast (8)
Apartment door opened to welcome him (6)
Author (5)
Blue numbers burnt into flesh (6)
Called Ron-ron by his big sister Hannah (5)
Carried Fayge to Lillith's Cave (5)
Chaya's aunt (4)
Chaya's friend Rivka: Aunt ____ (3)
Chaya's home village before joining Gitl (6)
Chaya's uncle who fails to escape camp (6)
Christian holiday celebrated by Rosemary (6)
Cremated (9)
Done to Jews' hair (5)
Eight day Jewish festival held in December (8)
Fayge and Shmuel were to married under one (6)
Fayge's Polish village (5)
Fayge's rabbi father: Reb ____ (6)
Garbage pile where children hid (6)
Gas ovens: ____'s Cave (7)
God's canopy (3)
Grandpa Will and Grandma Belle's residence (5)
Hannah Stern's hometown: New ____ (8)
Hitler's plan to rid the world of Jews: ____ solution (5)
Jewish guide book (8)

Jews made to carry the corpses (9)
Kommando Wolfe as a boy: Grandpa ____ (4)
Little hats worn by men during ceremony (9)
Made Hannah's head hurt after she drank it (4)
Made to work hard at the camp (7)
Mass destruction of European Jews (9)
Matzoh wrapped in blue cloth and hidden (8)
Means order (5)
Nazi camp commandant (5)
Number of days spent in the cattle cars (4)
Number of villagers to survive camp (3)
Permitted according to Jewish law (6)
Rivka's kerchief (8)
Shmuel's fiance (5)
Showers were ice ____ (4)
Spoken and understood by Chaya Abramowicz (7)
Steal (8)
Tatooing pen did this to arm flesh (6)
Those taken to the fire (6)
Time travels to Polish village in 1940's (6)
To remember and tell so it won't happen again: bear ____ (7)
Used by a young Hannah to imitate her grandfather: blue ____ (3)
Warning sound to children to hide (8)
Where Aaron hid the afikoman: clothes ____ (6)

Devil's Arithmetic Word Search 2 Answer Key

- Angel of Death: ____ Ha-mavis (6)
- Annual Jewish feast (8)
- Apartment door opened to welcome him (6)
- Author (5)
- Blue numbers burnt into flesh (6)
- Called Ron-ron by his big sister Hannah (5)
- Carried Fayge to Lillith's Cave (5)
- Chaya's aunt (4)
- Chaya's friend Rivka: Aunt ____ (3)
- Chaya's home village before joining Gitl (6)
- Chaya's uncle who fails to escape camp (6)
- Christian holiday celebrated by Rosemary (6)
- Cremated (9)
- Done to Jews' hair (5)
- Eight day Jewish festival held in December (8)
- Fayge and Shmuel were to married under one (6)
- Fayge's Polish village (5)
- Fayge's rabbi father: Reb ____ (6)
- Garbage pile where children hid (6)
- Gas ovens: ____'s Cave (7)
- God's canopy (3)
- Grandpa Will and Grandma Belle's residence (5)
- Hannah Stern's hometown: New ____ (8)
- Hitler's plan to rid the world of Jews: ____ solution (5)
- Jewish guide book (8)
- Jews made to carry the corpses (9)
- Kommando Wolfe as a boy: Grandpa ____ (4)
- Little hats worn by men during ceremony (9)
- Made Hannah's head hurt after she drank it (4)
- Made to work hard at the camp (7)
- Mass destruction of European Jews (9)
- Matzoh wrapped in blue cloth and hidden (8)
- Means order (5)
- Nazi camp commandant (5)
- Number of days spent in the cattle cars (4)
- Number of villagers to survive camp (3)
- Permitted according to Jewish law (6)
- Rivka's kerchief (8)
- Shmuel's fiance (5)
- Showers were ice ____ (4)
- Spoken and understood by Chaya Abramowicz (7)
- Steal (8)
- Tatooing pen did this to arm flesh (6)
- Those taken to the fire (6)
- Time travels to Polish village in 1940's (6)
- To remember and tell so it won't happen again: bear ____ (7)
- Used by a young Hannah to imitate her grandfather: blue ____ (3)
- Warning sound to children to hide (8)
- Where Aaron hid the afikoman: clothes ____ (6)

Devil's Arithmetic Word Search 3

```
H A G G A D A H R Q C T B U R N E D
O B R O N X A N V R N E O W M E C Y
L K O M M A N D O S L G L O T S K D
O W I T N E S S R C Q I H E D S Y S
C G B D F Q P R H S J H U L A H M H
A W B D S A M Y E H A N M B E S D R
U B R B Y Z Y J L Z H N H K L W O J
S R E H S O K G L R B N S J J I N G
T M U S S E L M E N A A A R O N L Z
Z Q R R Y G Y V E C V H B L N I S R
K M U A F R O D L E F I T U K P X D
K O S Z R S D T Z C V E O C S Q F H
F D T H S I D D I Y K N U S T H E R
W L Y A M M T S F S X L C E K S K A
W O P F T F W H F C H H D S S C C L
L I L L I T H B M N C G E W H O A L
T N N F I S N O L R E A I C R I O N
W K V E E K A O L L T O T T L S O Y
B O R U C H H L A L R I V H L E P G
Y O L E N S F M T P Z H C S K N Y V
```

AARON   COLD   KOMMANDOS   SHMUEL

ARITHMETIC   EASTER   KOSHER   SHORN

BABUSHKA   ELIJAH   LILLITH   SKY

BASKET   EVA   LUBLIN   TATTOO

BORUCH   FAYGE   MALACH   TWO

BREUR   FINAL   MIDDEN   VIOSK

BRONX   FOUR   MUSSELMEN   WILL

BURNED   GITL   PASSOVER   WINE

CANOPY   HAGGADAH   PROCESSED   WITNESS

CAULDRONS   HANNAH   ROCHELLE   WOLFE

CHOSEN   HOLOCAUST   SCHNELL   YIDDISH

CLUCKING   INK   SEDER   YOLEN

Devil's Arithmetic Word Search 3 Answer Key

AARON	COLD	KOMMANDOS	SHMUEL
ARITHMETIC	EASTER	KOSHER	SHORN
BABUSHKA	ELIJAH	LILLITH	SKY
BASKET	EVA	LUBLIN	TATTOO
BORUCH	FAYGE	MALACH	TWO
BREUR	FINAL	MIDDEN	VIOSK
BRONX	FOUR	MUSSELMEN	WILL
BURNED	GITL	PASSOVER	WINE
CANOPY	HAGGADAH	PROCESSED	WITNESS
CAULDRONS	HANNAH	ROCHELLE	WOLFE
CHOSEN	HOLOCAUST	SCHNELL	YIDDISH
CLUCKING	INK	SEDER	YOLEN

Devil's Arithmetic Word Search 4

```
A F I K O M A N I L B U L C H H E D
C A M X W R B Q N B M A A G T G
H K R J T O T K C B C N Y R N H
O O Y O H Y B S F B U K A U B E G
S S V S N X R N T W N A F E V A M Q
E H B W K V N I S A H E R Y L B E D
N E M D X Y E K H J F B T B U L F
K R L U L W D C S B T F H L K S T P
L O S K E T S U K R A Y G X Q H T D
C E E G Q L W L W O F S E M U K E B
C F D V I C A C H N R N K M E A S Q
B L E T R T L O V X I L M E S H E Q
B O R U C H L L I W H E A S I H E R N
W W O N A O O Z O X I M W I I Y E B
B F T J C K W U S R Y T L K O I V R
K N I A R F S G K P M L N W N D O M
K L U V S G I A O B I E P E S D S G
E S M I D D E N G S L C L W S I S K
T A T T O O A G A Y O N P F K Y S A K
B M A L A C H I Y L D L W K M H P F
```

AARON   COLD   KOSHER   SKY

AFIKOMAN   EASTER   LILLITH   SWALLOWS

BABUSHKA   ELIJAH   LUBLIN   TATTOO

BASKET   EVA   MALACH   TWO

BORUCH   FAYGE   MIDDEN   VIOSK

BREUR   FINAL   PASSOVER   WILL

BRONX   FOUR   QUESTIONS   WINE

BURNED   GITL   RESETTLEMENT   WITNESS

CANOPY   HANNAH   SCHNELL   WOLFE

CHANUKAH   HEALTHY   SEDER   YIDDISH

CHOSEN   HOLOCAUST   SHMUEL   YOLEN

CLUCKING   INK   SHORN   ZUGANGI

Devil's Arithmetic Word Search 4 Answer Key

```
A F I K O M A N I L B U L      H H E
C A         W   R            A A G T
H K   R     T O B     C      K N R N H
O O         H   U     H    N Y U B E
S S         N   R   H   N  A F E V A M
E H         K   N   A   H  E R   L B E
N   M D       Y E   K   B  L T     U L
    L U       D S   C   R  H L     S T
  C E G     L W A   L   O    Q     H T
    S D     I A L   O   N    U     K E
    E E     R L L   V   X    E     A S
B   R U     C   O   I   W    S     H E
  W O   J   A   W   O        T     E R
    F   A   C   S   S        I     Y E
K N I   A F S   G   K   P    O     D V
  L U       I   A   O   I    N     D O
E S M I D D E N   G A   L    S     I S
T A T T O O A     A   L      S     S A
  M A L A C H I   Y L                P
```

AARON   COLD   KOSHER   SKY

AFIKOMAN   EASTER   LILLITH   SWALLOWS

BABUSHKA   ELIJAH   LUBLIN   TATTOO

BASKET   EVA   MALACH   TWO

BORUCH   FAYGE   MIDDEN   VIOSK

BREUR   FINAL   PASSOVER   WILL

BRONX   FOUR   QUESTIONS   WINE

BURNED   GITL   RESETTLEMENT   WITNESS

CANOPY   HANNAH   SCHNELL   WOLFE

CHANUKAH   HEALTHY   SEDER   YIDDISH

CHOSEN   HOLOCAUST   SHMUEL   YOLEN

CLUCKING   INK   SHORN   ZUGANGI

Devil's Arithmetic Crossword 1

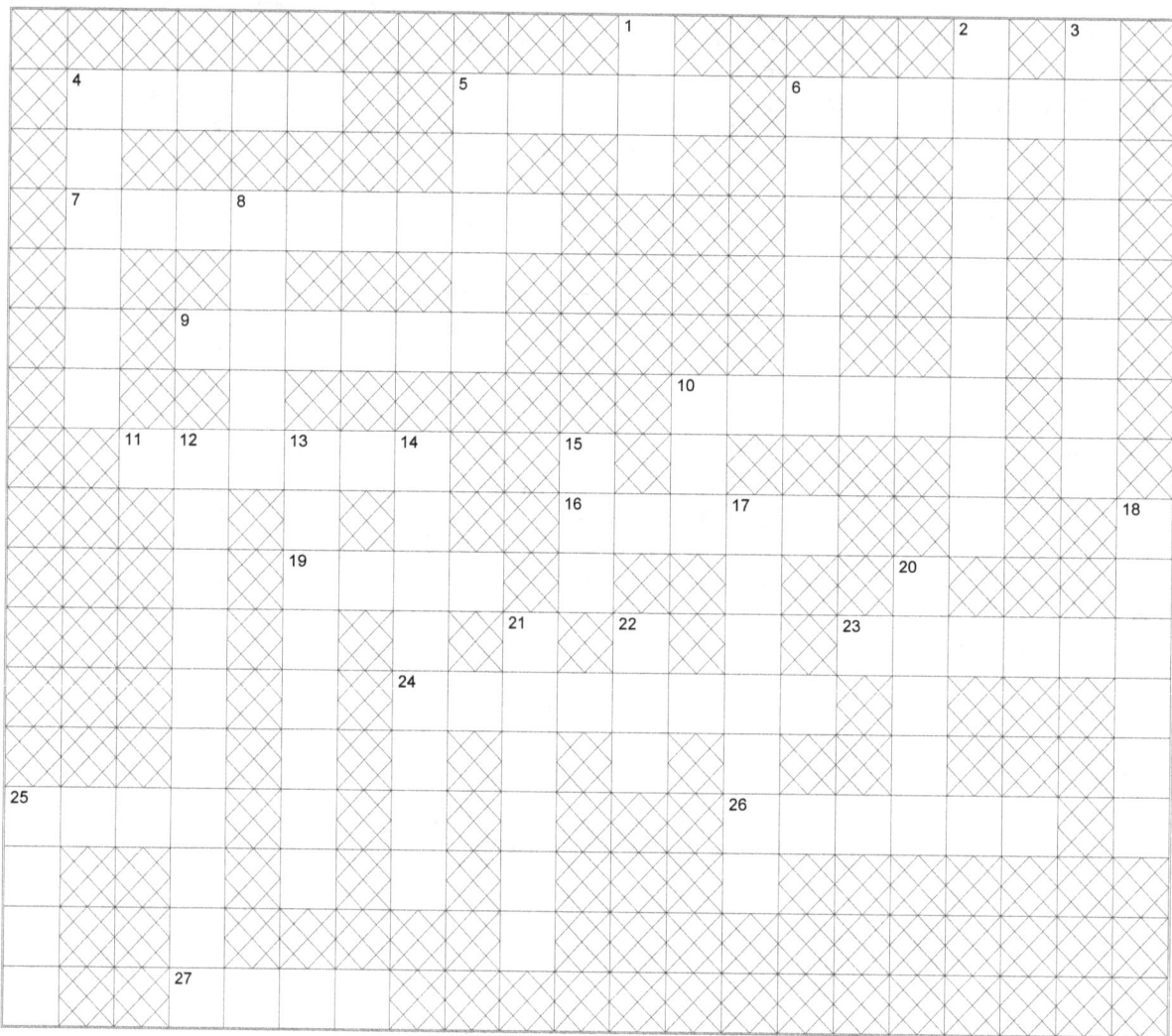

Across
4. Means order
5. Grandpa Will and Grandma Belle's residence
6. Fayge's rabbi father: Reb ___
7. Those who give up the fight
9. Permitted according to Jewish law
10. Blue numbers burnt into flesh
11. Fayge and Shmuel were to married under one
16. Fayge's Polish village
19. Chaya's aunt
23. Garbage pile where children hid
24. Warning sound to children to hide
25. Made Hannah's head hurt after she drank it
26. Chaya's home village before joining Gitl
27. Showers were ice ___

Down
1. Used by a young Hannah to imitate her grandfather: blue ___
2. Read by Aaron out of the Haggadah for the Seder: four ___
3. Eight day Jewish festival held in December
4. Chaya's uncle who fails to escape camp
5. Nazi camp commandant
6. Where Aaron hid the afikoman: clothes ___
8. Done to Jews' hair
10. Number of villagers to survive camp
12. One plus one; each day alive
13. Steal
14. Butcher who escaped camp
15. Chaya's friend Rivka: Aunt ___
17. Yelled constantly to the Jews at the camp
18. Time travels to Polish village in 1940's
20. Hitler's plan to rid the world of Jews: ___ solution
21. Tatooing pen did this to arm flesh
22. God's canopy
25. Kommando Wolfe as a boy: Grandpa ___

Devil's Arithmetic Crossword 1 Answer Key

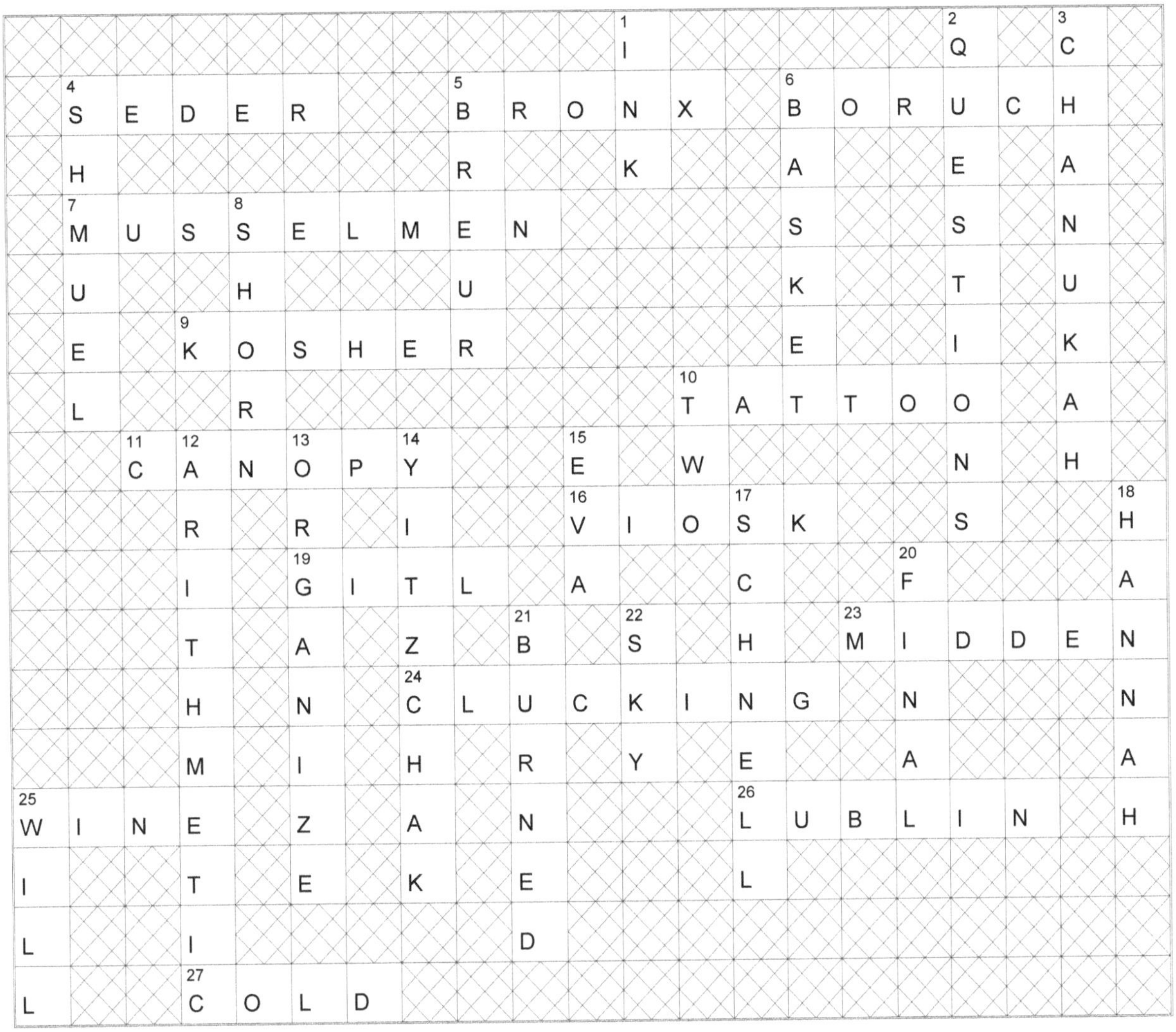

							1 I				2 Q		3 C
4 S	E	D	E	R		5 B	R	O	N	X	6 B	O	R	U	C	H

Row 1: _, _, _, _, _, _, _, 1-I, _, _, _, 2-Q, _, 3-C
Row 2: 4-S, E, D, E, R, _, 5-B, R, O, N, X, 6-B, O, R, U, C, H
Row 3: H, _, _, _, _, _, R, _, K, _, _, A, _, E, _, _, A
Row 4: 7-M, U, S, 8-S, E, L, M, E, N, _, _, S, _, S, _, _, N
Row 5: U, _, _, H, _, _, U, _, _, _, _, K, _, T, _, _, U
Row 6: E, _, 9-K, O, S, H, E, R, _, _, _, E, _, I, _, _, K
Row 7: L, _, _, _, _, _, _, _, _, _, 10-T, A, T, T, O, O, A
Row 8: _, 11-C, 12-A, N, 13-O, P, 14-Y, _, 15-E, W, _, _, _, N, _, H
Row 9: _, _, R, _, R, _, I, 16-V, I, O, 17-S, K, _, S, _, 18-H
Row 10: _, _, I, 19-G, I, T, L, A, _, _, C, _, 20-F, _, _, A
Row 11: _, _, T, _, A, _, Z, 21-B, 22-S, _, H, 23-M, I, D, D, E, N
Row 12: _, _, H, N, _, 24-C, L, U, C, K, I, N, G, _, _, N
Row 13: _, _, M, _, I, _, H, R, Y, _, E, _, A, _, _, A
Row 14: 25-W, I, N, E, Z, A, N, _, _, 26-L, U, B, L, I, N, H
Row 15: I, _, T, _, E, K, E, _, _, L, _, _, _, _, _, _
Row 16: L, _, I, _, _, _, D, _, _, _, _, _, _, _, _, _
Row 17: L, _, 27-C, O, L, D

Across
4. Means order
5. Grandpa Will and Grandma Belle's residence
6. Fayge's rabbi father: Reb ___
7. Those who give up the fight
9. Permitted according to Jewish law
10. Blue numbers burnt into flesh
11. Fayge and Shmuel were to married under one
16. Fayge's Polish village
19. Chaya's aunt
23. Garbage pile where children hid
24. Warning sound to children to hide
25. Made Hannah's head hurt after she drank it
26. Chaya's home village before joining Gitl
27. Showers were ice ___

Down
1. Used by a young Hannah to imitate her grandfather: blue ___
2. Read by Aaron out of the Haggadah for the Seder: four ___
3. Eight day Jewish festival held in December
4. Chaya's uncle who fails to escape camp
5. Nazi camp commandant
6. Where Aaron hid the afikoman: clothes ___
8. Done to Jews' hair
10. Number of villagers to survive camp
12. One plus one; each day alive
13. Steal
14. Butcher who escaped camp
15. Chaya's friend Rivka: Aunt ___
17. Yelled constantly to the Jews at the camp
18. Time travels to Polish village in 1940's
20. Hitler's plan to rid the world of Jews: ___ solution
21. Tatooing pen did this to arm flesh
22. God's canopy
25. Kommando Wolfe as a boy: Grandpa ___

Devil's Arithmetic Crossword 2

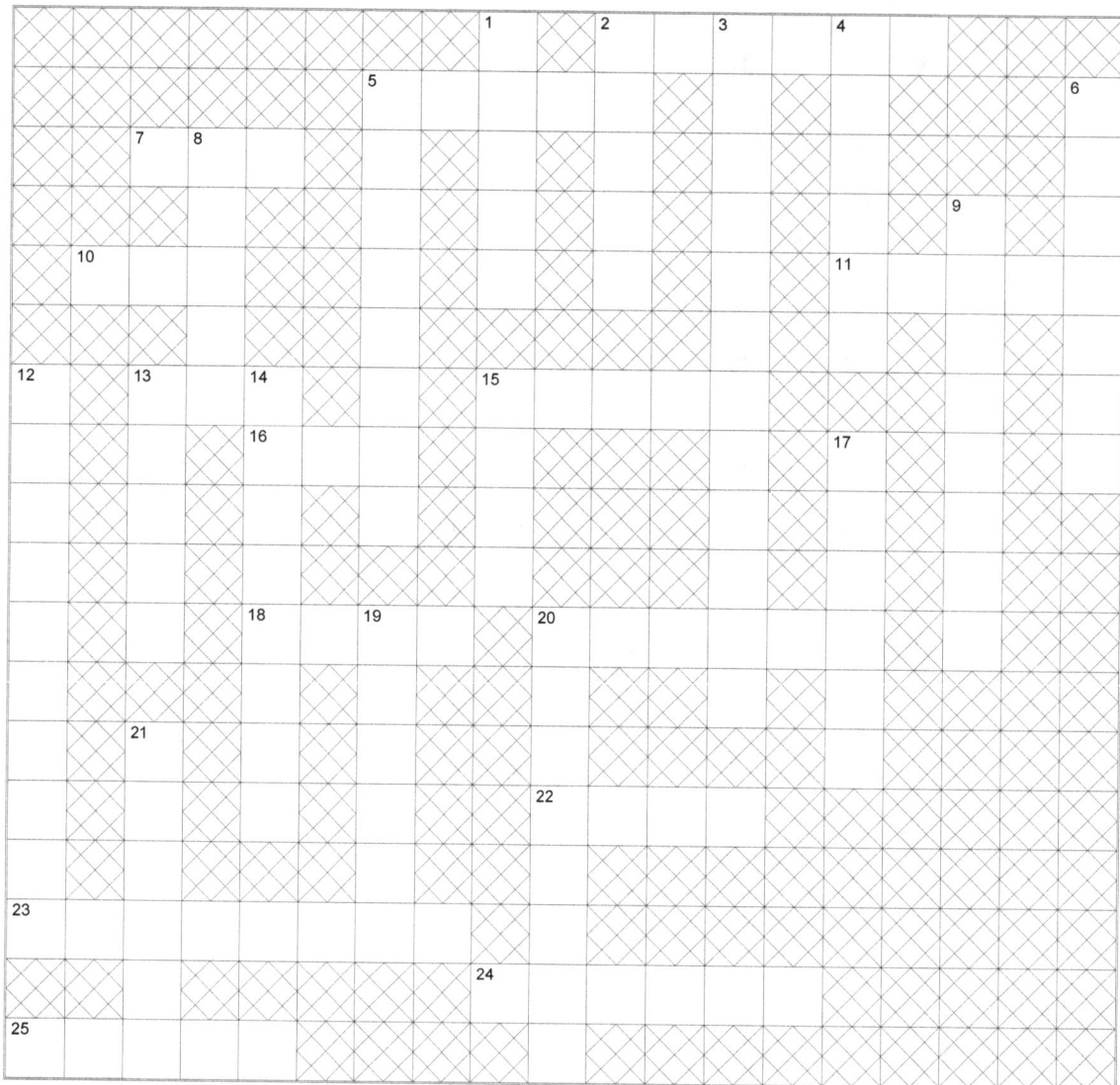

Across
2. Tatooing pen did this to arm flesh
5. Nazi camp commandant
7. Chaya's friend Rivka: Aunt ___
10. Number of villagers to survive camp
11. Called Ron-ron by his big sister Hannah
13. God's canopy
15. Hitler's plan to rid the world of Jews: ____ solution
16. Used by a young Hannah to imitate her grandfather: blue ___
18. Showers were ice ____
20. Time travels to Polish village in 1940's
22. Chaya's aunt
23. Warning sound to children to hide
24. Fayge and Shmuel were to married under one
25. Author

Down
1. Means order
2. Grandpa Will and Grandma Belle's residence
3. Removing Jews to the concentration camps
4. Apartment door opened to welcome him
5. Rivka's kerchief
6. Yelled constantly to the Jews at the camp
8. Fayge's Polish village
9. Steal
12. One plus one; each day alive
13. Done to Jews' hair
14. Butcher who escaped camp
15. Number of days spent in the cattle cars
17. Permitted according to Jewish law
19. Chaya's home village before joining Gitl
20. Jewish guide book
21. Chaya's uncle who fails to escape camp

Devil's Arithmetic Crossword 2 Answer Key

Across
2. Tatooing pen did this to arm flesh
5. Nazi camp commandant
7. Chaya's friend Rivka: Aunt ___
10. Number of villagers to survive camp
11. Called Ron-ron by his big sister Hannah
13. God's canopy
15. Hitler's plan to rid the world of Jews: ____ solution
16. Used by a young Hannah to imitate her grandfather: blue ___
18. Showers were ice ____
20. Time travels to Polish village in 1940's
22. Chaya's aunt
23. Warning sound to children to hide
24. Fayge and Shmuel were to married under one
25. Author

Down
1. Means order
2. Grandpa Will and Grandma Belle's residence
3. Removing Jews to the concentration camps
4. Apartment door opened to welcome him
5. Rivka's kerchief
6. Yelled constantly to the Jews at the camp
8. Fayge's Polish village
9. Steal
12. One plus one; each day alive
13. Done to Jews' hair
14. Butcher who escaped camp
15. Number of days spent in the cattle cars
17. Permitted according to Jewish law
19. Chaya's home village before joining Gitl
20. Jewish guide book
21. Chaya's uncle who fails to escape camp

Devil's Arithmetic Crossword 3

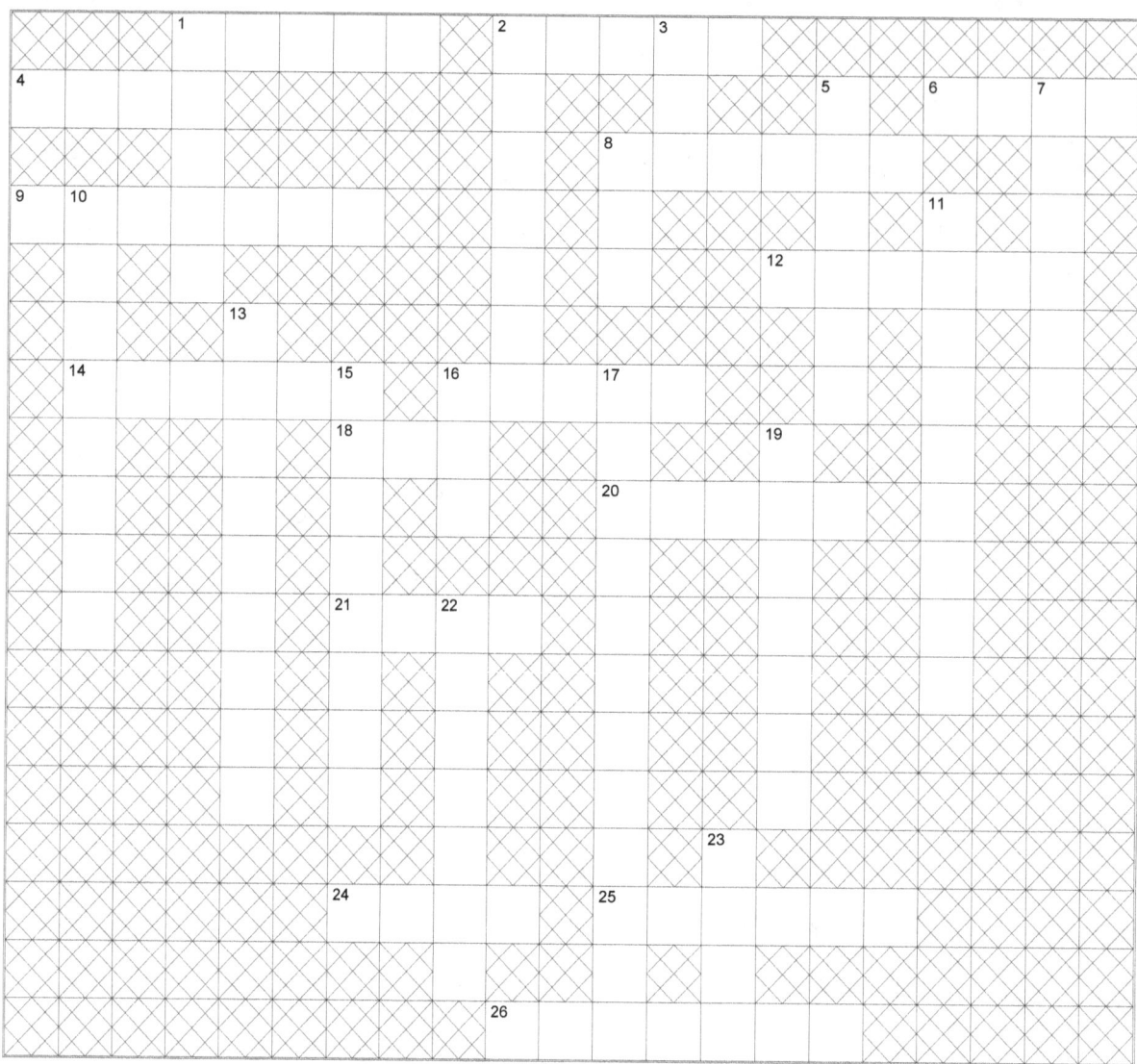

Across
1. Nazi camp commandant
2. Author
4. Number of days spent in the cattle cars
6. Kommando Wolfe as a boy: Grandpa ___
8. Blue numbers burnt into flesh
9. Yelled constantly to the Jews at the camp
12. Chaya's uncle who fails to escape camp
14. Fayge and Shmuel were to married under one
16. Done to Jews' hair
18. Used by a young Hannah to imitate her grandfather: blue ___
20. Means order
21. Showers were ice ____
24. Chaya's aunt
25. Apartment door opened to welcome him
26. To remember and tell so it won't happen again: bear ___

Down
1. Grandpa Will and Grandma Belle's residence
2. Spoken and understood by Chaya Abramowicz
3. Chaya's friend Rivka: Aunt ___
5. Permitted according to Jewish law
7. Chaya's home village before joining Gitl
8. Number of villagers to survive camp
10. Warning sound to children to hide
11. Those who give up the fight
13. Jews made to carry the corpses
15. Butcher who escaped camp
16. God's canopy
17. Removing Jews to the concentration camps
19. Made to work hard at the camp
22. Gas ovens: ____'s Cave
23. Made Hannah's head hurt after she drank it

Devil's Arithmetic Crossword 3 Answer Key

			¹B	R	E	U	R		²Y	O	³L	E	N				
⁴F	O	U	R						I		V			⁵K		⁶W	I	⁷L	L
			O					⁸T	A	T	T	O	O					U
⁹S	¹⁰C	H	N	E	L	L			D		W			S		¹¹M	B
	L		X						I		O		¹²S	H	M	U	E	L
	U			¹³K					S					E		S		I
	¹⁴C	A	N	O	P	¹⁵Y		¹⁶S	H	O	¹⁷R	N		R		S		N
	K					¹⁸I	N	K			E		¹⁹H		E		
	I					M						²⁰S	E	D	E	R		L
	N					M		T			Y		E		A		M	
	G					A		Z					T		L		E	
						N		²¹C	O	²²L	D		T				E	
						D		H		I			T		T		N	
						O		A		L			L		H			
						S		K		L			E		Y			
								I				²³W		
							²⁴G	I	T	L		²⁵E	L	I	J	A	H
								H				N			N		
						²⁶W	I	T	N	E	S	S

Across
1. Nazi camp commandant
2. Author
4. Number of days spent in the cattle cars
6. Kommando Wolfe as a boy: Grandpa ___
8. Blue numbers burnt into flesh
9. Yelled constantly to the Jews at the camp
12. Chaya's uncle who fails to escape camp
14. Fayge and Shmuel were to married under one
16. Done to Jews' hair
18. Used by a young Hannah to imitate her grandfather: blue ___
20. Means order
21. Showers were ice ___
24. Chaya's aunt
25. Apartment door opened to welcome him
26. To remember and tell so it won't happen again: bear ___

Down
1. Grandpa Will and Grandma Belle's residence
2. Spoken and understood by Chaya Abramowicz
3. Chaya's friend Rivka: Aunt ___
5. Permitted according to Jewish law
7. Chaya's home village before joining Gitl
8. Number of villagers to survive camp
10. Warning sound to children to hide
11. Those who give up the fight
13. Jews made to carry the corpses
15. Butcher who escaped camp
16. God's canopy
17. Removing Jews to the concentration camps
19. Made to work hard at the camp
22. Gas ovens: ___'s Cave
23. Made Hannah's head hurt after she drank it

Devil's Arithmetic Crossword 4

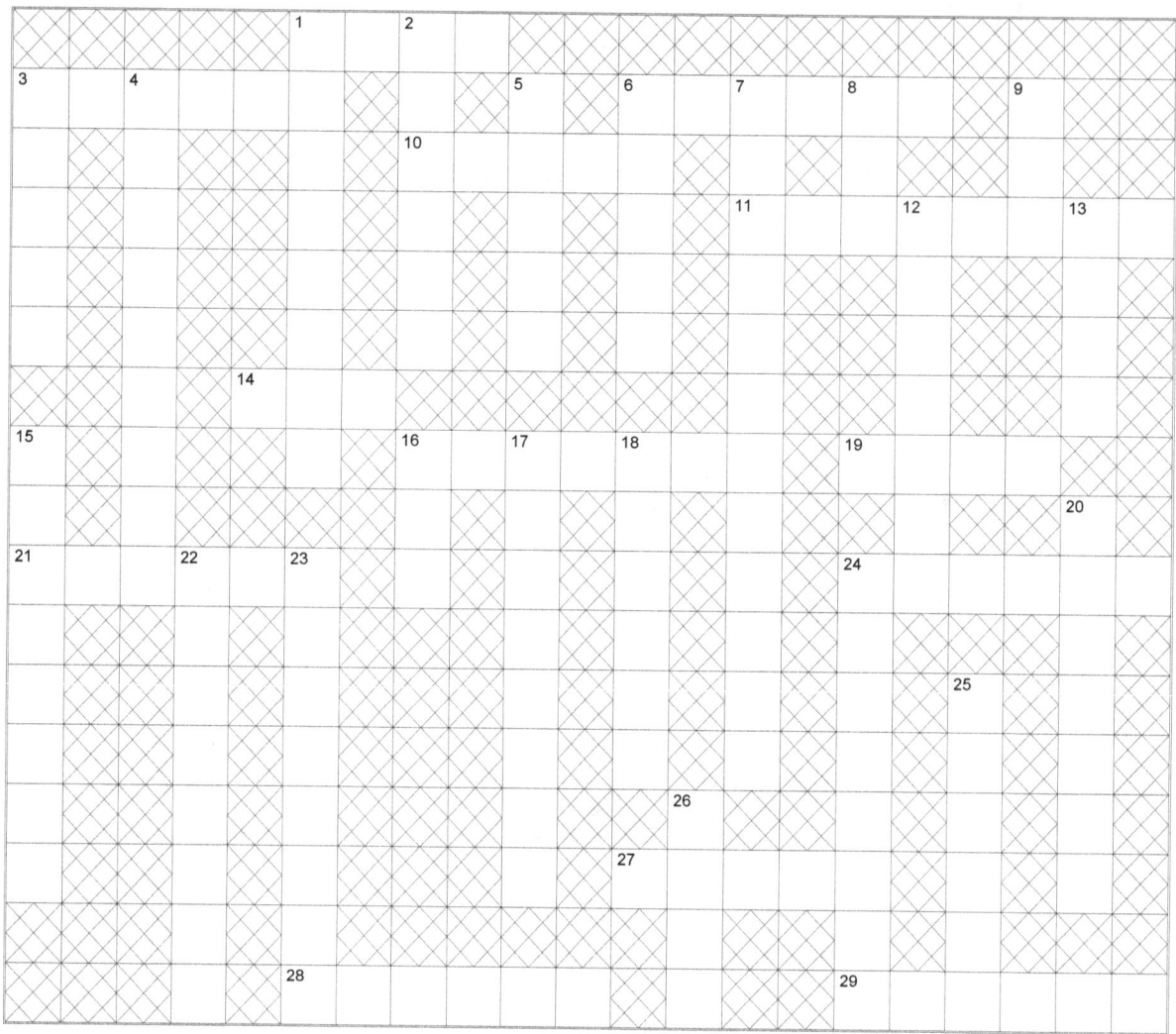

Across
1. Showers were ice ____
3. Chaya's uncle who fails to escape camp
6. Tatooing pen did this to arm flesh
10. Nazi camp commandant
11. Sang around the smokestack
14. Used by a young Hannah to imitate her grandfather: blue ___
16. Yelled constantly to the Jews at the camp
19. Chaya's aunt
21. Fayge and Shmuel were to married under one
24. Those taken to the fire
27. Fayge's Polish village
28. Permitted according to Jewish law
29. Time travels to Polish village in 1940's

Down
1. Warning sound to children to hide
2. Chaya's home village before joining Gitl
3. Done to Jews' hair
4. Those who give up the fight
5. Means order
6. Grandpa Will and Grandma Belle's residence
7. Removing Jews to the concentration camps
8. Chaya's friend Rivka: Aunt ___
9. Number of villagers to survive camp
12. Gas ovens: ____'s Cave
13. Kommando Wolfe as a boy: Grandpa ___
15. Hannah Stern's hometown: New ___
16. God's canopy
17. Jewish guide book
18. Apartment door opened to welcome him
20. Made to work hard at the camp
22. Steal
23. Butcher who escaped camp
24. Eight day Jewish festival held in December
25. Garbage pile where children hid
26. Made Hannah's head hurt after she drank it

Devil's Arithmetic Crossword 4 Answer Key

Across
1. Showers were ice ____
3. Chaya's uncle who fails to escape camp
6. Tatooing pen did this to arm flesh
10. Nazi camp commandant
11. Sang around the smokestack
14. Used by a young Hannah to imitate her grandfather: blue ____
16. Yelled constantly to the Jews at the camp
19. Chaya's aunt
21. Fayge and Shmuel were to married under one
24. Those taken to the fire
27. Fayge's Polish village
28. Permitted according to Jewish law
29. Time travels to Polish village in 1940's

Down
1. Warning sound to children to hide
2. Chaya's home village before joining Gitl
3. Done to Jews' hair
4. Those who give up the fight
5. Means order
6. Grandpa Will and Grandma Belle's residence
7. Removing Jews to the concentration camps
8. Chaya's friend Rivka: Aunt ____
9. Number of villagers to survive camp
12. Gas ovens: ____'s Cave
13. Kommando Wolfe as a boy: Grandpa ____
15. Hannah Stern's hometown: New ____
16. God's canopy
17. Jewish guide book
18. Apartment door opened to welcome him
20. Made to work hard at the camp
22. Steal
23. Butcher who escaped camp
24. Eight day Jewish festival held in December
25. Garbage pile where children hid
26. Made Hannah's head hurt after she drank it

Devil's Arithmetic

BASKET	BREUR	YOLEN	ARITHMETIC	LUBLIN
AARON	SCHNELL	LILLITH	CHOSEN	QUESTIONS
RESETTLEMENT	MALACH	FREE SPACE	KOMMANDOS	KOSHER
SKY	CHANUKAH	ORGANIZE	YARMULKES	BRONX
INK	WILL	YIDDISH	ELIJAH	TWO

Devil's Arithmetic

CLUCKING	YITZCHAK	MUSSELMEN	FAYGE	COLD
BABUSHKA	ZUGANGI	SHMUEL	ROCHELLE	BORUCH
WOLFE	AFIKOMAN	FREE SPACE	HANNAH	TATTOO
CANOPY	BURNED	CAULDRONS	SWALLOWS	EVA
HAGGADAH	HOLOCAUST	MIDDEN	WINE	FOUR

Devil's Arithmetic

FOUR	MALACH	EASTER	SWALLOWS	KOSHER
SCHNELL	COLD	SKY	YOLEN	QUESTIONS
FAYGE	AFIKOMAN	FREE SPACE	SEDER	TWO
WINE	INK	PASSOVER	CAULDRONS	CHOSEN
KOMMANDOS	BURNED	CHANUKAH	BRONX	BASKET

Devil's Arithmetic

BREUR	YARMULKES	ARITHMETIC	HOLOCAUST	CLUCKING
GITL	LILLITH	PROCESSED	WITNESS	ORGANIZE
YITZCHAK	BABUSHKA	FREE SPACE	WILL	WOLFE
MIDDEN	CANOPY	FINAL	EVA	ROCHELLE
SHMUEL	ZUGANGI	SHORN	HEALTHY	AARON

Devil's Arithmetic

FOUR	EASTER	EVA	WILL	HEALTHY
COLD	WOLFE	GITL	ARITHMETIC	YARMULKES
TATTOO	SWALLOWS	FREE SPACE	VIOSK	HANNAH
BRONX	BORUCH	YIDDISH	AARON	BASKET
QUESTIONS	MALACH	LILLITH	AFIKOMAN	YITZCHAK

Devil's Arithmetic

MUSSELMEN	TWO	BURNED	WINE	SEDER
BABUSHKA	KOMMANDOS	KOSHER	SHMUEL	ROCHELLE
RESETTLEMENT	CHANUKAH	FREE SPACE	BREUR	WITNESS
CANOPY	PROCESSED	INK	SKY	SCHNELL
CAULDRONS	SHORN	CHOSEN	FAYGE	ELIJAH

Devil's Arithmetic

EVA	WILL	SHMUEL	ZUGANGI	CAULDRONS
LILLITH	BREUR	SHORN	HEALTHY	YARMULKES
MALACH	TATTOO	FREE SPACE	SCHNELL	BASKET
FOUR	AFIKOMAN	YOLEN	FAYGE	CLUCKING
CHOSEN	HAGGADAH	BORUCH	MIDDEN	WINE

Devil's Arithmetic

BABUSHKA	SWALLOWS	ARITHMETIC	QUESTIONS	FINAL
PROCESSED	AARON	SKY	EASTER	COLD
CANOPY	MUSSELMEN	FREE SPACE	GITL	INK
KOSHER	PASSOVER	YITZCHAK	HOLOCAUST	VIOSK
BRONX	ROCHELLE	SEDER	RESETTLEMENT	YIDDISH

Devil's Arithmetic

ZUGANGI	QUESTIONS	WITNESS	HEALTHY	ROCHELLE
CAULDRONS	ARITHMETIC	PROCESSED	VIOSK	FINAL
HANNAH	FAYGE	FREE SPACE	YITZCHAK	WINE
CHOSEN	BURNED	EASTER	ELIJAH	MALACH
CLUCKING	HOLOCAUST	YARMULKES	ORGANIZE	GITL

Devil's Arithmetic

INK	MIDDEN	COLD	BRONX	WOLFE
EVA	BASKET	YIDDISH	CHANUKAH	SCHNELL
LUBLIN	BORUCH	FREE SPACE	BABUSHKA	KOMMANDOS
KOSHER	RESETTLEMENT	LILLITH	WILL	PASSOVER
FOUR	HAGGADAH	SWALLOWS	TWO	AFIKOMAN

Devil's Arithmetic

LUBLIN	AFIKOMAN	WOLFE	SKY	PROCESSED
AARON	RESETTLEMENT	FAYGE	FOUR	CHOSEN
ARITHMETIC	SWALLOWS	FREE SPACE	ORGANIZE	WILL
HANNAH	VIOSK	MIDDEN	HOLOCAUST	TWO
CAULDRONS	LILLITH	ROCHELLE	KOSHER	BURNED

Devil's Arithmetic

FINAL	EASTER	BORUCH	BABUSHKA	INK
GITL	TATTOO	CLUCKING	SCHNELL	ELIJAH
SHMUEL	WITNESS	FREE SPACE	QUESTIONS	MUSSELMEN
SHORN	EVA	MALACH	HEALTHY	COLD
WINE	YOLEN	HAGGADAH	YARMULKES	BASKET

Devil's Arithmetic

BABUSHKA	LUBLIN	MALACH	SWALLOWS	GITL
SHORN	VIOSK	LILLITH	MIDDEN	COLD
ROCHELLE	BRONX	FREE SPACE	PASSOVER	AARON
KOMMANDOS	SHMUEL	PROCESSED	BREUR	CANOPY
ZUGANGI	SCHNELL	HOLOCAUST	WITNESS	EASTER

Devil's Arithmetic

CAULDRONS	HANNAH	CHOSEN	HAGGADAH	RESETTLEMENT
HEALTHY	YITZCHAK	WILL	AFIKOMAN	ARITHMETIC
YOLEN	ELIJAH	FREE SPACE	KOSHER	TWO
WOLFE	SEDER	YARMULKES	TATTOO	BORUCH
FAYGE	CHANUKAH	FINAL	BURNED	FOUR

Devil's Arithmetic

ROCHELLE	FAYGE	ARITHMETIC	WINE	KOSHER
MIDDEN	MALACH	BABUSHKA	YOLEN	INK
GITL	WILL	FREE SPACE	HEALTHY	BURNED
EVA	ZUGANGI	COLD	MUSSELMEN	TWO
WITNESS	FOUR	CANOPY	SWALLOWS	LUBLIN

Devil's Arithmetic

HANNAH	YARMULKES	SCHNELL	BASKET	CAULDRONS
SKY	ORGANIZE	BORUCH	KOMMANDOS	TATTOO
SHMUEL	PASSOVER	FREE SPACE	RESETTLEMENT	SHORN
EASTER	FINAL	PROCESSED	YITZCHAK	CHOSEN
AFIKOMAN	QUESTIONS	BREUR	WOLFE	LILLITH

Devil's Arithmetic

QUESTIONS	PASSOVER	TWO	FOUR	WITNESS
CHANUKAH	EVA	COLD	CANOPY	ARITHMETIC
ELIJAH	BRONX	FREE SPACE	GITL	CHOSEN
BORUCH	HAGGADAH	INK	BREUR	EASTER
ROCHELLE	PROCESSED	AARON	RESETTLEMENT	FINAL

Devil's Arithmetic

WINE	LUBLIN	WOLFE	YIDDISH	AFIKOMAN
LILLITH	KOMMANDOS	WILL	VIOSK	KOSHER
MIDDEN	HOLOCAUST	FREE SPACE	HEALTHY	CLUCKING
SCHNELL	MALACH	YITZCHAK	YOLEN	SKY
ORGANIZE	BASKET	SEDER	SWALLOWS	SHMUEL

Devil's Arithmetic

GITL	EASTER	ORGANIZE	AFIKOMAN	ELIJAH
TWO	SHORN	MALACH	MIDDEN	LILLITH
BRONX	CHOSEN	FREE SPACE	YIDDISH	FAYGE
SKY	PASSOVER	YITZCHAK	SCHNELL	ZUGANGI
WOLFE	WINE	COLD	BREUR	HAGGADAH

Devil's Arithmetic

HANNAH	YOLEN	TATTOO	CANOPY	CHANUKAH
ARITHMETIC	WILL	KOMMANDOS	ROCHELLE	BABUSHKA
INK	CLUCKING	FREE SPACE	SHMUEL	SWALLOWS
FINAL	WITNESS	YARMULKES	HEALTHY	BORUCH
AARON	RESETTLEMENT	HOLOCAUST	MUSSELMEN	QUESTIONS

Devil's Arithmetic

CHOSEN	HANNAH	FOUR	SHORN	ZUGANGI
AFIKOMAN	QUESTIONS	HAGGADAH	BASKET	ROCHELLE
HOLOCAUST	YOLEN	FREE SPACE	CANOPY	BURNED
SCHNELL	MIDDEN	ELIJAH	BORUCH	VIOSK
GITL	KOSHER	KOMMANDOS	COLD	INK

Devil's Arithmetic

RESETTLEMENT	FAYGE	TATTOO	AARON	BRONX
LUBLIN	PASSOVER	PROCESSED	ARITHMETIC	YARMULKES
BREUR	WINE	FREE SPACE	EVA	MALACH
SHMUEL	CHANUKAH	FINAL	SKY	EASTER
ORGANIZE	HEALTHY	YITZCHAK	LILLITH	WITNESS

Devil's Arithmetic

SCHNELL	BASKET	WINE	MUSSELMEN	YIDDISH
CANOPY	WILL	FOUR	BABUSHKA	MALACH
RESETTLEMENT	GITL	FREE SPACE	TATTOO	YITZCHAK
FINAL	YARMULKES	PROCESSED	CAULDRONS	HOLOCAUST
FAYGE	BORUCH	SWALLOWS	WITNESS	PASSOVER

Devil's Arithmetic

COLD	SHMUEL	QUESTIONS	HEALTHY	MIDDEN
SHORN	LUBLIN	ORGANIZE	TWO	KOMMANDOS
VIOSK	EVA	FREE SPACE	INK	AFIKOMAN
WOLFE	CLUCKING	CHOSEN	ROCHELLE	CHANUKAH
LILLITH	BURNED	KOSHER	SEDER	ZUGANGI

Devil's Arithmetic

BURNED	HEALTHY	SHMUEL	SHORN	EVA
KOSHER	CAULDRONS	FINAL	SKY	SCHNELL
MUSSELMEN	ELIJAH	FREE SPACE	WOLFE	TATTOO
TWO	EASTER	HOLOCAUST	YITZCHAK	LUBLIN
CANOPY	MALACH	LILLITH	VIOSK	YIDDISH

Devil's Arithmetic

PROCESSED	QUESTIONS	YARMULKES	ARITHMETIC	SWALLOWS
BRONX	RESETTLEMENT	BASKET	ZUGANGI	CLUCKING
BREUR	WINE	FREE SPACE	ORGANIZE	KOMMANDOS
AARON	MIDDEN	FAYGE	HAGGADAH	PASSOVER
GITL	COLD	WILL	BABUSHKA	AFIKOMAN

Devil's Arithmetic

WOLFE	TWO	RESETTLEMENT	PASSOVER	BREUR
SHMUEL	SWALLOWS	HANNAH	YITZCHAK	ROCHELLE
SKY	MIDDEN	FREE SPACE	CAULDRONS	KOSHER
EVA	BRONX	BABUSHKA	LUBLIN	FOUR
ARITHMETIC	QUESTIONS	ZUGANGI	BASKET	TATTOO

Devil's Arithmetic

KOMMANDOS	SHORN	WINE	PROCESSED	CHOSEN
ELIJAH	HOLOCAUST	YOLEN	AFIKOMAN	SCHNELL
ORGANIZE	HEALTHY	FREE SPACE	GITL	MALACH
FINAL	FAYGE	CANOPY	LILLITH	EASTER
CLUCKING	VIOSK	WILL	BURNED	HAGGADAH

Devil's Arithmetic

ARITHMETIC	SKY	GITL	KOSHER	WINE
LUBLIN	YIDDISH	BRONX	INK	HEALTHY
BORUCH	FOUR	FREE SPACE	BABUSHKA	YARMULKES
BASKET	CANOPY	PROCESSED	FINAL	EVA
MIDDEN	BREUR	SCHNELL	YITZCHAK	MUSSELMEN

Devil's Arithmetic

VIOSK	ELIJAH	SEDER	SWALLOWS	BURNED
TATTOO	SHMUEL	RESETTLEMENT	ZUGANGI	ORGANIZE
QUESTIONS	PASSOVER	FREE SPACE	CHANUKAH	WILL
EASTER	KOMMANDOS	COLD	CHOSEN	AARON
WOLFE	FAYGE	CLUCKING	YOLEN	ROCHELLE

Devil's Arithmetic

LUBLIN	RESETTLEMENT	BREUR	YITZCHAK	TATTOO
SHORN	WOLFE	INK	PROCESSED	MUSSELMEN
EVA	AFIKOMAN	FREE SPACE	ELIJAH	KOSHER
AARON	BASKET	COLD	YIDDISH	FOUR
GITL	HAGGADAH	CHANUKAH	SEDER	YOLEN

Devil's Arithmetic

SKY	WITNESS	MIDDEN	BURNED	MALACH
VIOSK	LILLITH	ARITHMETIC	EASTER	BABUSHKA
TWO	SWALLOWS	FREE SPACE	CANOPY	PASSOVER
ORGANIZE	SHMUEL	WINE	FAYGE	ROCHELLE
WILL	SCHNELL	HEALTHY	HANNAH	BORUCH

Devil's Arithmetic Vocabulary Word List

No.	Word	Clue/Definition
1.	AFFIRMATION	Approval
2.	ALIENATED	Distances
3.	AMALGAM	Mixture
4.	APPALLED	Shocked
5.	ARBITRARY	Erratic; inconsistent
6.	BILLET	Position
7.	BURNISHED	Polished; waxed
8.	CLOYING	Satisfying
9.	COMPANIONABLE	Friendly; agreeable
10.	COMPENSATION	Benefits
11.	COMPRESSION	Reduction
12.	CONSPIRATORIAL	Secretly plotting
13.	CREMATORIA	Furnace used for cremation
14.	DECREED	Ordered
15.	DEHUMANIZED	Deprived of human dignity
16.	DESECRATE	Ruin; violate
17.	DISCERNIBLE	Recognizable
18.	DISSIPATING	Disappearing
19.	DISTORTED	Deformed; twisted
20.	DOUR	Sour; gloomy
21.	ELUSIVE	Puzzling; slippery
22.	EXODUS	Departure; exit
23.	FERVOR	Heated emotion
24.	GARISH	Tasteless; gaudy
25.	GAUDY	Showy
26.	GRUESOME	Horrible
27.	GUTTURAL	Throaty; gravelly
28.	IMPUDENT	Cocky; arrogant
29.	INCINERATION	Burning
30.	INDELIBLE	Permanent; unforgetting
31.	INGRATE	Ungrateful person
32.	IRONY	Contradiction
33.	JOSTLING	Bouncing; bumping
34.	LUCID	Clear-headed
35.	LUMINOUS	Bright; shining
36.	MEAGER	Skimpy
37.	MESMERIZED	Hypnotized; captivated
38.	MORTIFIED	Humiliated
39.	OMINOUS	Threatening
40.	PERIPHERY	Edge; fringe
41.	PERVASIVE	Widespread
42.	PORTENTS	Indications; omens
43.	PROFOUND	Heavy; penetrating
44.	RAUCOUS	Loud; piercing
45.	RELENTLESSLY	Steadily; constantly
46.	RIVETED	Attention drawn to
47.	ROUTINIZATION	Put into a system
48.	SATANIC	Of Satan
49.	SLOVENS	Unclean; untidy
50.	SONOROUS	Deep; full sounded
51.	STACCATO	Loud, abrupt sounds

Devil's Arithmetic Vocabulary Word List Continued

No.	Word	Clue/Definition
52.	SUPERIMPOSED	One image on top of another
53.	TIMIDITY	Shyness
54.	UNCOMPREHENDINGLY	Without understanding
55.	UNDECIPHERABLE	Unable to solve
56.	UNDISTINGUISHABLE	Unable to distinguish
57.	UNLEAVENED	Made without yeast
58.	VEHEMENCE	Passion; intensity
59.	VIGOR	Energy
60.	VULNERABLE	Defenseless; exposed

Copyrighted

Devil's Arithmetic Vocabulary Fill In The Blank 1

_____ 1. One image on top of another
_____ 2. Defenseless; exposed
_____ 3. Cocky; arrogant
_____ 4. Recognizable
_____ 5. Horrible
_____ 6. Put into a system
_____ 7. Unable to solve
_____ 8. Disappearing
_____ 9. Edge; fringe
_____ 10. Shyness
_____ 11. Distances
_____ 12. Deep; full sounded
_____ 13. Of Satan
_____ 14. Furnace used for cremation
_____ 15. Steadily; constantly
_____ 16. Burning
_____ 17. Bright; shining
_____ 18. Contradiction
_____ 19. Loud, abrupt sounds
_____ 20. Satisfying

Devil's Arithmetic Vocabulary Fill In The Blank 1 Answer Key

SUPERIMPOSED	1. One image on top of another
VULNERABLE	2. Defenseless; exposed
IMPUDENT	3. Cocky; arrogant
DISCERNIBLE	4. Recognizable
GRUESOME	5. Horrible
ROUTINIZATION	6. Put into a system
UNDECIPHERABLE	7. Unable to solve
DISSIPATING	8. Disappearing
PERIPHERY	9. Edge; fringe
TIMIDITY	10. Shyness
ALIENATED	11. Distances
SONOROUS	12. Deep; full sounded
SATANIC	13. Of Satan
CREMATORIA	14. Furnace used for cremation
RELENTLESSLY	15. Steadily; constantly
INCINERATION	16. Burning
LUMINOUS	17. Bright; shining
IRONY	18. Contradiction
STACCATO	19. Loud, abrupt sounds
CLOYING	20. Satisfying

Devil's Arithmetic Vocabulary Fill In The Blank 2

_____ 1. Burning

_____ 2. Approval

_____ 3. Departure; exit

_____ 4. Unclean; untidy

_____ 5. Defenseless; exposed

_____ 6. Secretly plotting

_____ 7. Widespread

_____ 8. Loud, abrupt sounds

_____ 9. Puzzling; slippery

_____ 10. Benefits

_____ 11. Ruin; violate

_____ 12. Edge; fringe

_____ 13. Erratic; inconsistent

_____ 14. Steadily; constantly

_____ 15. Permanent; unforgetting

_____ 16. Attention drawn to

_____ 17. Deprived of human dignity

_____ 18. Bouncing; bumping

_____ 19. Bright; shining

_____ 20. Unable to distinguish

Devil's Arithmetic Vocabulary Fill In The Blank 2 Answer Key

INCINERATION	1.	Burning
AFFIRMATION	2.	Approval
EXODUS	3.	Departure; exit
SLOVENS	4.	Unclean; untidy
VULNERABLE	5.	Defenseless; exposed
CONSPIRATORIAL	6.	Secretly plotting
PERVASIVE	7.	Widespread
STACCATO	8.	Loud, abrupt sounds
ELUSIVE	9.	Puzzling; slippery
COMPENSATION	10.	Benefits
DESECRATE	11.	Ruin; violate
PERIPHERY	12.	Edge; fringe
ARBITRARY	13.	Erratic; inconsistent
RELENTLESSLY	14.	Steadily; constantly
INDELIBLE	15.	Permanent; unforgetting
RIVETED	16.	Attention drawn to
DEHUMANIZED	17.	Deprived of human dignity
JOSTLING	18.	Bouncing; bumping
LUMINOUS	19.	Bright; shining
UNDISTINGUISHABLE	20.	Unable to distinguish

Devil's Arithmetic Vocabulary Fill In The Blank 3

_____ 1. Put into a system

_____ 2. Deformed; twisted

_____ 3. Loud; piercing

_____ 4. Furnace used for cremation

_____ 5. Ungrateful person

_____ 6. Friendly; agreeable

_____ 7. Approval

_____ 8. Energy

_____ 9. Without understanding

_____ 10. Threatening

_____ 11. Benefits

_____ 12. Sour; gloomy

_____ 13. Recognizable

_____ 14. Passion; intensity

_____ 15. Shyness

_____ 16. Shocked

_____ 17. Indications; omens

_____ 18. Hypnotized; captivated

_____ 19. Made without yeast

_____ 20. Polished; waxed

Devil's Arithmetic Vocabulary Fill In The Blank 3 Answer Key

ROUTINIZATION	1. Put into a system
DISTORTED	2. Deformed; twisted
RAUCOUS	3. Loud; piercing
CREMATORIA	4. Furnace used for cremation
INGRATE	5. Ungrateful person
COMPANIONABLE	6. Friendly; agreeable
AFFIRMATION	7. Approval
VIGOR	8. Energy
UNCOMPREHENDINGLY	9. Without understanding
OMINOUS	10. Threatening
COMPENSATION	11. Benefits
DOUR	12. Sour; gloomy
DISCERNIBLE	13. Recognizable
VEHEMENCE	14. Passion; intensity
TIMIDITY	15. Shyness
APPALLED	16. Shocked
PORTENTS	17. Indications; omens
MESMERIZED	18. Hypnotized; captivated
UNLEAVENED	19. Made without yeast
BURNISHED	20. Polished; waxed

Devil's Arithmetic Vocabulary Fill In The Blank 4

_____ 1. Distances
_____ 2. Attention drawn to
_____ 3. Shocked
_____ 4. Reduction
_____ 5. Made without yeast
_____ 6. Position
_____ 7. Defenseless; exposed
_____ 8. Mixture
_____ 9. Cocky; arrogant
_____ 10. Bright; shining
_____ 11. Satisfying
_____ 12. Steadily; constantly
_____ 13. Ruin; violate
_____ 14. Burning
_____ 15. Passion; intensity
_____ 16. Heavy; penetrating
_____ 17. Of Satan
_____ 18. Hypnotized; captivated
_____ 19. Horrible
_____ 20. Approval

Devil's Arithmetic Vocabulary Fill In The Blank 4 Answer key

ALIENATED	1.	Distances
RIVETED	2.	Attention drawn to
APPALLED	3.	Shocked
COMPRESSION	4.	Reduction
UNLEAVENED	5.	Made without yeast
BILLET	6.	Position
VULNERABLE	7.	Defenseless; exposed
AMALGAM	8.	Mixture
IMPUDENT	9.	Cocky; arrogant
LUMINOUS	10.	Bright; shining
CLOYING	11.	Satisfying
RELENTLESSLY	12.	Steadily; constantly
DESECRATE	13.	Ruin; violate
INCINERATION	14.	Burning
VEHEMENCE	15.	Passion; intensity
PROFOUND	16.	Heavy; penetrating
SATANIC	17.	Of Satan
MESMERIZED	18.	Hypnotized; captivated
GRUESOME	19.	Horrible
AFFIRMATION	20.	Approval

Devil's Arithmetic Vocabulary Matching 1

___ 1. CREMATORIA   A. Polished; waxed
___ 2. PORTENTS   B. Disappearing
___ 3. AFFIRMATION   C. Ordered
___ 4. FERVOR   D. One image on top of another
___ 5. INCINERATION   E. Furnace used for cremation
___ 6. INGRATE   F. Unclean; untidy
___ 7. MEAGER   G. Of Satan
___ 8. UNLEAVENED   H. Defenseless; exposed
___ 9. DISCERNIBLE   I. Permanent; unforgetting
___10. VULNERABLE   J. Ungrateful person
___11. SLOVENS   K. Humiliated
___12. DISSIPATING   L. Approval
___13. ROUTINIZATION   M. Heavy; penetrating
___14. PROFOUND   N. Bright; shining
___15. SATANIC   O. Skimpy
___16. DECREED   P. Erratic; inconsistent
___17. ARBITRARY   Q. Made without yeast
___18. LUMINOUS   R. Deformed; twisted
___19. UNDISTINGUISHABLE   S. Recognizable
___20. UNCOMPREHENDINGLY   T. Without understanding
___21. INDELIBLE   U. Heated emotion
___22. SUPERIMPOSED   V. Unable to distinguish
___23. BURNISHED   W. Put into a system
___24. DISTORTED   X. Indications; omens
___25. MORTIFIED   Y. Burning

Devil's Arithmetic Vocabulary Matching 1 Answer Key

E - 1. CREMATORIA   A. Polished; waxed
X - 2. PORTENTS   B. Disappearing
L - 3. AFFIRMATION   C. Ordered
U - 4. FERVOR   D. One image on top of another
Y - 5. INCINERATION   E. Furnace used for cremation
J - 6. INGRATE   F. Unclean; untidy
O - 7. MEAGER   G. Of Satan
Q - 8. UNLEAVENED   H. Defenseless; exposed
S - 9. DISCERNIBLE   I. Permanent; unforgetting
H -10. VULNERABLE   J. Ungrateful person
F -11. SLOVENS   K. Humiliated
B -12. DISSIPATING   L. Approval
W -13. ROUTINIZATION   M. Heavy; penetrating
M -14. PROFOUND   N. Bright; shining
G -15. SATANIC   O. Skimpy
C -16. DECREED   P. Erratic; inconsistent
P -17. ARBITRARY   Q. Made without yeast
N -18. LUMINOUS   R. Deformed; twisted
V -19. UNDISTINGUISHABLE   S. Recognizable
T -20. UNCOMPREHENDINGLY   T. Without understanding
I -21. INDELIBLE   U. Heated emotion
D -22. SUPERIMPOSED   V. Unable to distinguish
A -23. BURNISHED   W. Put into a system
R -24. DISTORTED   X. Indications; omens
K -25. MORTIFIED   Y. Burning

Devil's Arithmetic Vocabulary Matching 2

___ 1. ARBITRARY   A. Ruin; violate
___ 2. RIVETED   B. Polished; waxed
___ 3. GRUESOME   C. Disappearing
___ 4. JOSTLING   D. Skimpy
___ 5. LUMINOUS   E. Attention drawn to
___ 6. BILLET   F. Shyness
___ 7. DESECRATE   G. Satisfying
___ 8. CLOYING   H. Hypnotized; captivated
___ 9. TIMIDITY   I. Clear-headed
___10. DECREED   J. Permanent; unforgetting
___11. RAUCOUS   K. Made without yeast
___12. AMALGAM   L. Loud; piercing
___13. PROFOUND   M. Bouncing; bumping
___14. LUCID   N. Edge; fringe
___15. BURNISHED   O. Position
___16. INDELIBLE   P. Ordered
___17. ALIENATED   Q. Bright; shining
___18. DISSIPATING   R. Horrible
___19. MESMERIZED   S. Erratic; inconsistent
___20. DISCERNIBLE   T. Widespread
___21. PERIPHERY   U. Mixture
___22. UNLEAVENED   V. Humiliated
___23. PERVASIVE   W. Recognizable
___24. MORTIFIED   X. Distances
___25. MEAGER   Y. Heavy; penetrating

Devil's Arithmetic Vocabulary Matching 2 Answer Key

S - 1. ARBITRARY		A. Ruin; violate
E - 2. RIVETED		B. Polished; waxed
R - 3. GRUESOME		C. Disappearing
M - 4. JOSTLING		D. Skimpy
Q - 5. LUMINOUS		E. Attention drawn to
O - 6. BILLET		F. Shyness
A - 7. DESECRATE		G. Satisfying
G - 8. CLOYING		H. Hypnotized; captivated
F - 9. TIMIDITY		I. Clear-headed
P - 10. DECREED		J. Permanent; unforgetting
L - 11. RAUCOUS		K. Made without yeast
U - 12. AMALGAM		L. Loud; piercing
Y - 13. PROFOUND		M. Bouncing; bumping
I - 14. LUCID		N. Edge; fringe
B - 15. BURNISHED		O. Position
J - 16. INDELIBLE		P. Ordered
X - 17. ALIENATED		Q. Bright; shining
C - 18. DISSIPATING		R. Horrible
H - 19. MESMERIZED		S. Erratic; inconsistent
W - 20. DISCERNIBLE		T. Widespread
N - 21. PERIPHERY		U. Mixture
K - 22. UNLEAVENED		V. Humiliated
T - 23. PERVASIVE		W. Recognizable
V - 24. MORTIFIED		X. Distances
D - 25. MEAGER		Y. Heavy; penetrating

Copyrighted

Devil's Arithmetic Vocabulary Matching 3

___ 1. COMPANIONABLE   A. Threatening
___ 2. PROFOUND   B. Shyness
___ 3. STACCATO   C. Of Satan
___ 4. TIMIDITY   D. Recognizable
___ 5. SLOVENS   E. Unable to distinguish
___ 6. PERIPHERY   F. Energy
___ 7. UNLEAVENED   G. Horrible
___ 8. AMALGAM   H. Furnace used for cremation
___ 9. VIGOR   I. Unable to solve
___10. SONOROUS   J. Deep; full sounded
___11. GRUESOME   K. Disappearing
___12. DISSIPATING   L. Mixture
___13. GARISH   M. Loud, abrupt sounds
___14. OMINOUS   N. Heavy; penetrating
___15. DISCERNIBLE   O. Sour; gloomy
___16. DOUR   P. Unclean; untidy
___17. SATANIC   Q. Friendly; agreeable
___18. UNDECIPHERABLE   R. Made without yeast
___19. UNDISTINGUISHABLE S. Deprived of human dignity
___20. INDELIBLE   T. Tasteless; gaudy
___21. DEHUMANIZED   U. Edge; fringe
___22. CLOYING   V. Heated emotion
___23. CREMATORIA   W. Permanent; unforgetting
___24. DESECRATE   X. Satisfying
___25. FERVOR   Y. Ruin; violate

Devil's Arithmetic Vocabulary Matching 3 Answer Key

Q - 1. COMPANIONABLE   A. Threatening
N - 2. PROFOUND   B. Shyness
M - 3. STACCATO   C. Of Satan
B - 4. TIMIDITY   D. Recognizable
P - 5. SLOVENS   E. Unable to distinguish
U - 6. PERIPHERY   F. Energy
R - 7. UNLEAVENED   G. Horrible
L - 8. AMALGAM   H. Furnace used for cremation
F - 9. VIGOR   I. Unable to solve
J - 10. SONOROUS   J. Deep; full sounded
G - 11. GRUESOME   K. Disappearing
K - 12. DISSIPATING   L. Mixture
T - 13. GARISH   M. Loud, abrupt sounds
A - 14. OMINOUS   N. Heavy; penetrating
D - 15. DISCERNIBLE   O. Sour; gloomy
O - 16. DOUR   P. Unclean; untidy
C - 17. SATANIC   Q. Friendly; agreeable
I - 18. UNDECIPHERABLE   R. Made without yeast
E - 19. UNDISTINGUISHABLE   S. Deprived of human dignity
W - 20. INDELIBLE   T. Tasteless; gaudy
S - 21. DEHUMANIZED   U. Edge; fringe
X - 22. CLOYING   V. Heated emotion
H - 23. CREMATORIA   W. Permanent; unforgetting
Y - 24. DESECRATE   X. Satisfying
V - 25. FERVOR   Y. Ruin; violate

Devil's Arithmetic Vocabulary Matching 4

___ 1. VULNERABLE   A. Passion; intensity
___ 2. UNLEAVENED   B. Threatening
___ 3. ALIENATED   C. Secretly plotting
___ 4. DISSIPATING   D. Heated emotion
___ 5. DISTORTED   E. Unable to solve
___ 6. COMPRESSION   F. One image on top of another
___ 7. IRONY   G. Defenseless; exposed
___ 8. PERVASIVE   H. Widespread
___ 9. DESECRATE   I. Unclean; untidy
___ 10. UNDECIPHERABLE   J. Ruin; violate
___ 11. OMINOUS   K. Deformed; twisted
___ 12. CREMATORIA   L. Furnace used for cremation
___ 13. CONSPIRATORIAL   M. Approval
___ 14. BILLET   N. Contradiction
___ 15. VEHEMENCE   O. Reduction
___ 16. PROFOUND   P. Bright; shining
___ 17. LUMINOUS   Q. Hypnotized; captivated
___ 18. TIMIDITY   R. Shyness
___ 19. AFFIRMATION   S. Distances
___ 20. SLOVENS   T. Position
___ 21. FERVOR   U. Showy
___ 22. GAUDY   V. Made without yeast
___ 23. SONOROUS   W. Disappearing
___ 24. SUPERIMPOSED   X. Deep; full sounded
___ 25. MESMERIZED   Y. Heavy; penetrating

Devil's Arithmetic Vocabulary Matching 4 Answer Key

G - 1. VULNERABLE		A. Passion; intensity
V - 2. UNLEAVENED		B. Threatening
S - 3. ALIENATED		C. Secretly plotting
W - 4. DISSIPATING		D. Heated emotion
K - 5. DISTORTED		E. Unable to solve
O - 6. COMPRESSION		F. One image on top of another
N - 7. IRONY		G. Defenseless; exposed
H - 8. PERVASIVE		H. Widespread
J - 9. DESECRATE		I. Unclean; untidy
E - 10. UNDECIPHERABLE		J. Ruin; violate
B - 11. OMINOUS		K. Deformed; twisted
L - 12. CREMATORIA		L. Furnace used for cremation
C - 13. CONSPIRATORIAL		M. Approval
T - 14. BILLET		N. Contradiction
A - 15. VEHEMENCE		O. Reduction
Y - 16. PROFOUND		P. Bright; shining
P - 17. LUMINOUS		Q. Hypnotized; captivated
R - 18. TIMIDITY		R. Shyness
M - 19. AFFIRMATION		S. Distances
I - 20. SLOVENS		T. Position
D - 21. FERVOR		U. Showy
U - 22. GAUDY		V. Made without yeast
X - 23. SONOROUS		W. Disappearing
F - 24. SUPERIMPOSED		X. Deep; full sounded
Q - 25. MESMERIZED		Y. Heavy; penetrating

Copyrighted

Devil's Arithmetic Vocabulary Magic Squares 1

Match the definition with the vocabulary word. Put your answers in the magic squares below. When your answers are correct, all columns and rows will add to the same number.

A. IMPUDENT
B. ALIENATED
C. VEHEMENCE
D. INGRATE
E. FERVOR
F. PERVASIVE
G. UNDECIPHERABLE
H. MEAGER
I. RELENTLESSLY
J. PERIPHERY
K. GARISH
L. MESMERIZED
M. ELUSIVE
N. VIGOR
O. GAUDY
P. EXODUS

1. Passion; intensity
2. Edge; fringe
3. Widespread
4. Showy
5. Departure; exit
6. Heated emotion
7. Steadily; constantly
8. Ungrateful person
9. Puzzling; slippery
10. Skimpy
11. Hypnotized; captivated
12. Cocky; arrogant
13. Distances
14. Tasteless; gaudy
15. Unable to solve
16. Energy

A=	B=	C=	D=
E=	F=	G=	H=
I=	J=	K=	L=
M=	N=	O=	P=

Devil's Arithmetic Vocabulary Magic Squares 1 Answer Key

Match the definition with the vocabulary word. Put your answers in the magic squares below. When your answers are correct, all columns and rows will add to the same number.

A. IMPUDENT
B. ALIENATED
C. VEHEMENCE
D. INGRATE
E. FERVOR
F. PERVASIVE
G. UNDECIPHERABLE
H. MEAGER
I. RELENTLESSLY
J. PERIPHERY
K. GARISH
L. MESMERIZED
M. ELUSIVE
N. VIGOR
O. GAUDY
P. EXODUS

1. Passion; intensity
2. Edge; fringe
3. Widespread
4. Showy
5. Departure; exit
6. Heated emotion
7. Steadily; constantly
8. Ungrateful person
9. Puzzling; slippery
10. Skimpy
11. Hypnotized; captivated
12. Cocky; arrogant
13. Distances
14. Tasteless; gaudy
15. Unable to solve
16. Energy

A=12	B=13	C=1	D=8
E=6	F=3	G=15	H=10
I=7	J=2	K=14	L=11
M=9	N=16	O=4	P=5

Devil's Arithmetic Vocabulary Magic Squares 2

Match the definition with the vocabulary word. Put your answers in the magic squares below. When your answers are correct, all columns and rows will add to the same number.

A. UNDISTINGUISHABLE
B. GAUDY
C. VEHEMENCE
D. RIVETED
E. APPALLED
F. CONSPIRATORIAL
G. CLOYING
H. INCINERATION
I. COMPENSATION
J. IRONY
K. AMALGAM
L. SLOVENS
M. EXODUS
N. RAUCOUS
O. INGRATE
P. BILLET

1. Loud; piercing
2. Satisfying
3. Unclean; untidy
4. Unable to distinguish
5. Mixture
6. Showy
7. Departure; exit
8. Burning
9. Shocked
10. Position
11. Passion; intensity
12. Contradiction
13. Attention drawn to
14. Benefits
15. Secretly plotting
16. Ungrateful person

A=	B=	C=	D=
E=	F=	G=	H=
I=	J=	K=	L=
M=	N=	O=	P=

Devil's Arithmetic Vocabulary Magic Squares 2 Answer Key

Match the definition with the vocabulary word. Put your answers in the magic squares below. When your answers are correct, all columns and rows will add to the same number.

A. UNDISTINGUISHABLE
B. GAUDY
C. VEHEMENCE
D. RIVETED
E. APPALLED
F. CONSPIRATORIAL
G. CLOYING
H. INCINERATION
I. COMPENSATION
J. IRONY
K. AMALGAM
L. SLOVENS
M. EXODUS
N. RAUCOUS
O. INGRATE
P. BILLET

1. Loud; piercing
2. Satisfying
3. Unclean; untidy
4. Unable to distinguish
5. Mixture
6. Showy
7. Departure; exit
8. Burning
9. Shocked
10. Position
11. Passion; intensity
12. Contradiction
13. Attention drawn to
14. Benefits
15. Secretly plotting
16. Ungrateful person

A=4	B=6	C=11	D=13
E=9	F=15	G=2	H=8
I=14	J=12	K=5	L=3
M=7	N=1	O=16	P=10

Devil's Arithmetic Vocabulary Magic Squares 3

Match the definition with the vocabulary word. Put your answers in the magic squares below. When your answers are correct, all columns and rows will add to the same number.

A. BURNISHED
B. DISCERNIBLE
C. SATANIC
D. ELUSIVE
E. LUCID
F. INCINERATION
G. PERIPHERY
H. RAUCOUS
I. ROUTINIZATION
J. BILLET
K. ARBITRARY
L. GUTTURAL
M. DISTORTED
N. COMPRESSION
O. PERVASIVE
P. IMPUDENT

1. Deformed; twisted
2. Burning
3. Loud; piercing
4. Widespread
5. Throaty; gravelly
6. Of Satan
7. Polished; waxed
8. Position
9. Erratic; inconsistent
10. Puzzling; slippery
11. Recognizable
12. Put into a system
13. Reduction
14. Clear-headed
15. Edge; fringe
16. Cocky; arrogant

A=	B=	C=	D=
E=	F=	G=	H=
I=	J=	K=	L=
M=	N=	O=	P=

Devil's Arithmetic Vocabulary Magic Squares 3 Answer Key

Match the definition with the vocabulary word. Put your answers in the magic squares below. When your answers are correct, all columns and rows will add to the same number.

A. BURNISHED
B. DISCERNIBLE
C. SATANIC
D. ELUSIVE
E. LUCID
F. INCINERATION
G. PERIPHERY
H. RAUCOUS
I. ROUTINIZATION
J. BILLET
K. ARBITRARY
L. GUTTURAL
M. DISTORTED
N. COMPRESSION
O. PERVASIVE
P. IMPUDENT

1. Deformed; twisted
2. Burning
3. Loud; piercing
4. Widespread
5. Throaty; gravelly
6. Of Satan
7. Polished; waxed
8. Position
9. Erratic; inconsistent
10. Puzzling; slippery
11. Recognizable
12. Put into a system
13. Reduction
14. Clear-headed
15. Edge; fringe
16. Cocky; arrogant

A=7	B=11	C=6	D=10
E=14	F=2	G=15	H=3
I=12	J=8	K=9	L=5
M=1	N=13	O=4	P=16

Devil's Arithmetic Vocabulary Magic Squares 4

Match the definition with the vocabulary word. Put your answers in the magic squares below. When your answers are correct, all columns and rows will add to the same number.

A. GUTTURAL
B. DISSIPATING
C. PERIPHERY
D. VIGOR
E. OMINOUS
F. STACCATO
G. BILLET
H. INCINERATION
I. DOUR
J. ELUSIVE
K. VULNERABLE
L. PORTENTS
M. CLOYING
N. DEHUMANIZED
O. VEHEMENCE
P. EXODUS

1. Burning
2. Satisfying
3. Disappearing
4. Defenseless; exposed
5. Puzzling; slippery
6. Edge; fringe
7. Departure; exit
8. Threatening
9. Passion; intensity
10. Loud, abrupt sounds
11. Sour; gloomy
12. Energy
13. Throaty; gravelly
14. Indications; omens
15. Position
16. Deprived of human dignity

A=	B=	C=	D=
E=	F=	G=	H=
I=	J=	K=	L=
M=	N=	O=	P=

Devil's Arithmetic Vocabulary Magic Squares 4 Answer Key

Match the definition with the vocabulary word. Put your answers in the magic squares below. When your answers are correct, all columns and rows will add to the same number.

A. GUTTURAL
B. DISSIPATING
C. PERIPHERY
D. VIGOR
E. OMINOUS
F. STACCATO

G. BILLET
H. INCINERATION
I. DOUR
J. ELUSIVE
K. VULNERABLE
L. PORTENTS

M. CLOYING
N. DEHUMANIZED
O. VEHEMENCE
P. EXODUS

1. Burning
2. Satisfying
3. Disappearing
4. Defenseless; exposed
5. Puzzling; slippery
6. Edge; fringe
7. Departure; exit
8. Threatening
9. Passion; intensity
10. Loud, abrupt sounds
11. Sour; gloomy
12. Energy
13. Throaty; gravelly
14. Indications; omens
15. Position
16. Deprived of human dignity

A=13	B=3	C=6	D=12
E=8	F=10	G=15	H=1
I=11	J=5	K=4	L=14
M=2	N=16	O=9	P=7

Devil's Arithmetic Vocabulary Word Search 1

```
T N E D U P M I A D E C R E E D M L G M
I D M D F N G L M G V O F C I I E U U V
M N A E H M I X A L J M V S P S S M N P
I B I L L E T N L F K P C C E T M I D W
D Q R L N A P H G J S E I G R O E N I D
I F O A O G L L T R N R J I R R O S J
T M T P M E R M M N A S R H P T I U T K
Y E A P I R F X I T C A T R H E Z S I N
D Q M A N W T B A E U T E U E D E J N L
Q I E Z O H L S C C N I L O R G D O G K
T X R R U E R N O B C O B D Y U V S U V
K I C O S V E U T D E N I E M T N T I K
M P N N N M S V W S T F L N W T R L S Y
O Y K C E Y N U V N A S E E G U S I H D
R Y K H I S Y L D E R S D V M R K N A S
T X E Y Y N N N B V C N N A C A A G B T
I V Q P X V E E M O E K I E C L C T L D
F G F E R V O R Y L S S E L T N E L E R
I X A R Z Y O A A S E Y O N N V U T G B
E Q T R C G P B Z T D Y Z U I C E E A C
D B N F I C S L Z L I P Q S I V N X U N
V R G V P S L E F N Q O U D I P X O D M
X V K G N P H N G B J L N R T L M D Y C
S O N O R O U S S S E V E M O S E U R G
Q S W F X R D E S O P M I R E P U S T Q
```

Attention drawn to (7)
Benefits (12)
Bouncing; bumping (8)
Bright; shining (8)
Burning (12)
Clear-headed (5)
Cocky; arrogant (8)
Contradiction (5)
Deep; full sounded (8)
Defenseless; exposed (10)
Deformed; twisted (9)
Departure; exit (6)
Distances (9)
Edge; fringe (9)
Energy (5)
Furnace used for cremation (10)
Heated emotion (6)
Horrible (8)
Humiliated (9)
Hypnotized; captivated (10)
Loud; piercing (7)
Made without yeast (10)
Mixture (7)

Of Satan (7)
One image on top of another (12)
Ordered (7)
Passion; intensity (9)
Permanent; unforgetting (9)
Position (6)
Puzzling; slippery (7)
Recognizable (11)
Ruin; violate (9)
Satisfying (7)
Shocked (8)
Showy (5)
Shyness (8)
Skimpy (6)
Sour; gloomy (4)
Steadily; constantly (12)
Tasteless; gaudy (6)
Threatening (7)
Throaty; gravelly (8)
Unable to distinguish (17)
Unclean; untidy (7)
Ungrateful person (7)

Devil's Arithmetic Vocabulary Word Search 1 Answer Key

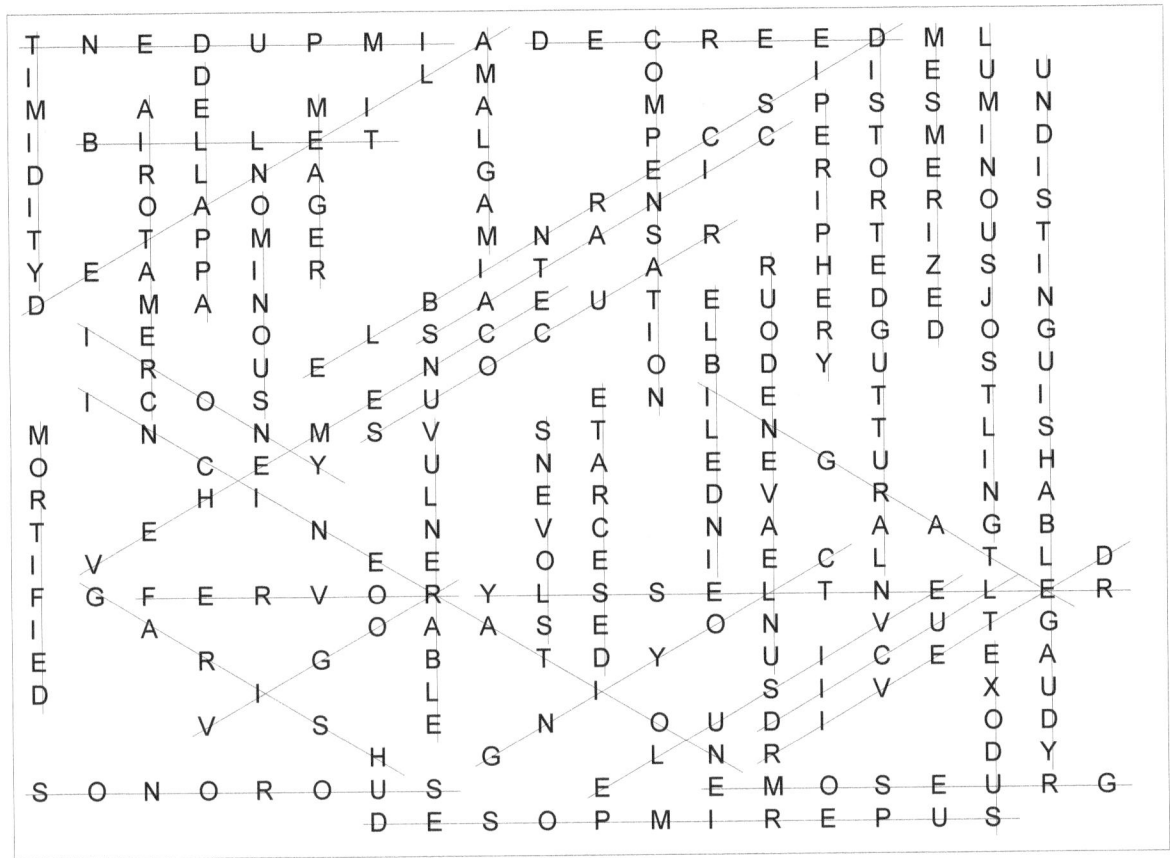

Attention drawn to (7)
Benefits (12)
Bouncing; bumping (8)
Bright; shining (8)
Burning (12)
Clear-headed (5)
Cocky; arrogant (8)
Contradiction (5)
Deep; full sounded (8)
Defenseless; exposed (10)
Deformed; twisted (9)
Departure; exit (6)
Distances (9)
Edge; fringe (9)
Energy (5)
Furnace used for cremation (10)
Heated emotion (6)
Horrible (8)
Humiliated (9)
Hypnotized; captivated (10)
Loud; piercing (7)
Made without yeast (10)
Mixture (7)

Of Satan (7)
One image on top of another (12)
Ordered (7)
Passion; intensity (9)
Permanent; unforgetting (9)
Position (6)
Puzzling; slippery (7)
Recognizable (11)
Ruin; violate (9)
Satisfying (7)
Shocked (8)
Showy (5)
Shyness (8)
Skimpy (6)
Sour; gloomy (4)
Steadily; constantly (12)
Tasteless; gaudy (6)
Threatening (7)
Throaty; gravelly (8)
Unable to distinguish (17)
Unclean; untidy (7)
Ungrateful person (7)

Devil's Arithmetic Vocabulary Word Search 2

```
A F F I R M A T I O N P R O F O U N D K
U R G N N K V P N D Q W W C D M I Z L J
S N B U H G L C P T Z S U O R O N O S G
L X C I T R P J A N Y F X N R C Y L H
O P W O T T O A W S L A R V G T I W N N
V V N G M R U R T M H L K G B I N Q X G
E M Y W T P A R Z E J I E K Y F E D L K
N Y B E F U R R A T Z E N D J I R E U M
S D N W C P E E Y L D N V V H E A T M J
V T D O B T L Y H E R A D O I D T E I P
S R U Y E L B M Z E H T K S M G I V N L
V S K L H D A I H R N E U V K I O I O R
Y E L B I N R E C S I D E H S I N R U B
R I V N G E E J R P O V I T V D V O S F
B Q E V M F N V H X I F A N E D D D U R
T P H S J Q L L E S J C R L G W S E F S
G I E C J Y U R U O C M I A S L F C E F
A M M R D Z V L S A J B S M A G Y R R H
U P E I I F E T T X L H J A T R M E V Y
D U N L D P L O K E Y S D L A U E E O C
Y D C H P I H C L O Y I N G N E A D R T
F E E M N R T E P C C R G A I S G Y C Z
Z N R G S O P Y R U M A L M C O E S V H
T T Q K L N K T L Y K G N D N M R P V J
F W P M D Y D I S T O R T E D E Q Z M K
```

Approval (11)

Attention drawn to (7)

Bouncing; bumping (8)

Bright; shining (8)

Burning (12)

Clear-headed (5)

Cocky; arrogant (8)

Contradiction (5)

Deep; full sounded (8)

Defenseless; exposed (10)

Deformed; twisted (9)

Departure; exit (6)

Distances (9)

Edge; fringe (9)

Energy (5)

Erratic; inconsistent (9)

Heated emotion (6)

Heavy; penetrating (8)

Horrible (8)

Humiliated (9)

Hypnotized; captivated (10)

Indications; omens (8)

Loud, abrupt sounds (8)

Loud; piercing (7)

Mixture (7)

Of Satan (7)

Ordered (7)

Passion; intensity (9)

Permanent; unforgetting (9)

Polished; waxed (9)

Position (6)

Puzzling; slippery (7)

Recognizable (11)

Satisfying (7)

Shocked (8)

Showy (5)

Shyness (8)

Skimpy (6)

Sour; gloomy (4)

Tasteless; gaudy (6)

Threatening (7)

Throaty; gravelly (8)

Unclean; untidy (7)

Ungrateful person (7)

Without understanding (17)

Devil's Arithmetic Vocabulary Word Search 2 Answer Key

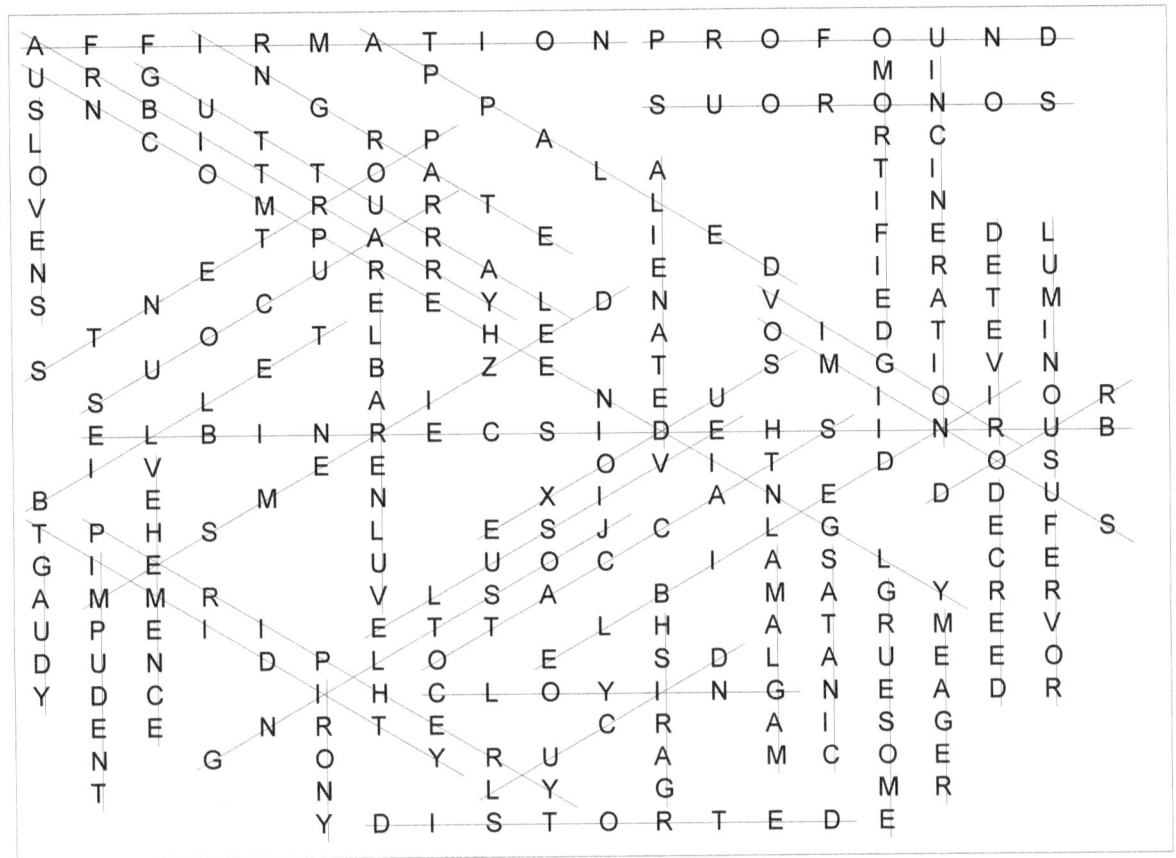

Approval (11)	Erratic; inconsistent (9)	Position (6)
Attention drawn to (7)	Heated emotion (6)	Puzzling; slippery (7)
Bouncing; bumping (8)	Heavy; penetrating (8)	Recognizable (11)
Bright; shining (8)	Horrible (8)	Satisfying (7)
Burning (12)	Humiliated (9)	Shocked (8)
Clear-headed (5)	Hypnotized; captivated (10)	Showy (5)
Cocky; arrogant (8)	Indications; omens (8)	Shyness (8)
Contradiction (5)	Loud, abrupt sounds (8)	Skimpy (6)
Deep; full sounded (8)	Loud; piercing (7)	Sour; gloomy (4)
Defenseless; exposed (10)	Mixture (7)	Tasteless; gaudy (6)
Deformed; twisted (9)	Of Satan (7)	Threatening (7)
Departure; exit (6)	Ordered (7)	Throaty; gravelly (8)
Distances (9)	Passion; intensity (9)	Unclean; untidy (7)
Edge; fringe (9)	Permanent; unforgetting (9)	Ungrateful person (7)
Energy (5)	Polished; waxed (9)	Without understanding (17)

Devil's Arithmetic Vocabulary Word Search 3

```
T F S R C O N S P I R A T O R I A L T L
A L I E A T E D A J O S T H L I N G U G
R Q C N M T D D N M V C F H Y K Z N E S
M P X W E N D L V A M O R T I F I E D P
K T H T H X U Z Q L R H I Y R C D L I H
P X R G S R O S Z G F D Q K C R L S G B
X O L B R C F B O A I G D B V L U T B Q
P G R U E S O M E M K D I U A M H A N F
R M O R C S R M I R I L L P I L U B G V
S K G N C I P T P S L N P N D O Q I U M
H L I I N L D F S E E A O C D M E T L N
Y Y V S E F O I T R N U X U H E L R I G
J Y G H B L P Y A M S S E Q S A B A S L
P Z X E H A U B I J E L A S W G I R H N
S E D D T Q L S G N B S K T D E L Y A X
T N R I Q E W U I A G D M E I R E D B Z
A I N V L S D D N V R P Z E D O D U L M
C G N G A E T O S L E I Q I R L N A E M
C R P G T S I X D O N W S S O I I G D Q
A M A E R N I E L A N T L H V R Z X D T
T H V U A A E V M M O O H D R O R E J K
O I J P C R T U E R V W R Z E N T J D V
R Q M P C O H E T E J N F O F Y T J N V
M O Y E Y E U E N P G U T T U R A L C N
C K D S D M D S A T A N I C P S X S Q N
```

ALIENATED	ELUSIVE	MORTIFIED
AMALGAM	EXODUS	OMINOUS
APPALLED	FERVOR	PERVASIVE
ARBITRARY	GARISH	PORTENTS
BILLET	GAUDY	PROFOUND
BURNISHED	GRUESOME	RAUCOUS
CLOYING	GUTTURAL	RIVETED
COMPANIONABLE	INDELIBLE	SATANIC
COMPENSATION	INGRATE	SLOVENS
CONSPIRATORIAL	IRONY	SONOROUS
DECREED	JOSTLING	STACCATO
DEHUMANIZED	LUCID	TIMIDITY
DISSIPATING	LUMINOUS	UNDISTINGUISHABLE
DISTORTED	MEAGER	VIGOR
DOUR	MESMERIZED	VULNERABLE

Devil's Arithmetic Vocabulary Word Search 3 Answer Key

ALIENATED
AMALGAM
APPALLED
ARBITRARY
BILLET
BURNISHED
CLOYING
COMPANIONABLE
COMPENSATION
CONSPIRATORIAL
DECREED
DEHUMANIZED
DISSIPATING
DISTORTED
DOUR

ELUSIVE
EXODUS
FERVOR
GARISH
GAUDY
GRUESOME
GUTTURAL
INDELIBLE
INGRATE
IRONY
JOSTLING
LUCID
LUMINOUS
MEAGER
MESMERIZED

MORTIFIED
OMINOUS
PERVASIVE
PORTENTS
PROFOUND
RAUCOUS
RIVETED
SATANIC
SLOVENS
SONOROUS
STACCATO
TIMIDITY
UNDISTINGUISHABLE
VIGOR
VULNERABLE

Devil's Arithmetic Vocabulary Word Search 4

```
D I N D E L I B L E I P J O S T L I N G
I D G E D X R L Q B M E S D W G V G P
S A R C O G Z P X B U P R L P P R H R
T L U D M M R K P R H N I O Q Q B X
O I E E C I S O O T N D P V C F N
R E S E A T N V U D R I S I E H E Z N
T N O D E R R O I T Q T M L S N E N M
E A M N V Z E B S U W I A E I G H T R S
D T E J A F L C I Z S G N X N D H E F Y
Q E C H E N E J C T L H Q I R T I F D Z
Y D X O L R S L A A R Z T C Z V S T T Y
S A T A N I C C M G A U D Y A J G Y R
Q B N I U S C M K P R R B F D T N B L
F K B P G A P F C I H V Q Y O S O I U W
M L P N T P N I S O J F V U E R L C O M
E D R O G I V S R R M O R T I F I E D N
A Y O I L Q I U Q A W P A A L D T H E B
G C F T V D S D L V T R R L U A V C P X
E E O A C E W O P N G O A E R C N B B G
R L U M L J T X N N E R R C S E O H Q P
J U N R O F V E I O U R E I M S S U Z R
X S D I Y Z Q T D T R S A E A I I H S H
H I G F I Q J Y T B E O H B R L V O H C
Q V V F N V G U N D B E U A L C M T N J
J E X A G L G J K G V Y G S T E L L I B
```

AFFIRMATION	DISSIPATING	INGRATE	ROUTINIZATION
ALIENATED	DISTORTED	IRONY	SATANIC
AMALGAM	DOUR	JOSTLING	SLOVENS
ARBITRARY	ELUSIVE	LUCID	SONOROUS
BILLET	EXODUS	MEAGER	STACCATO
BURNISHED	FERVOR	MORTIFIED	TIMIDITY
CLOYING	GARISH	OMINOUS	UNLEAVENED
COMPRESSION	GAUDY	PERIPHERY	VEHEMENCE
CONSPIRATORIAL	GRUESOME	PORTENTS	VIGOR
DECREED	GUTTURAL	PROFOUND	VULNERABLE
DESECRATE	IMPUDENT	RAUCOUS	
DISCERNIBLE	INDELIBLE	RIVETED	

Devil's Arithmetic Vocabulary Word Search 4 Answer Key

AFFIRMATION	DISSIPATING	INGRATE	ROUTINIZATION
ALIENATED	DISTORTED	IRONY	SATANIC
AMALGAM	DOUR	JOSTLING	SLOVENS
ARBITRARY	ELUSIVE	LUCID	SONOROUS
BILLET	EXODUS	MEAGER	STACCATO
BURNISHED	FERVOR	MORTIFIED	TIMIDITY
CLOYING	GARISH	OMINOUS	UNLEAVENED
COMPRESSION	GAUDY	PERIPHERY	VEHEMENCE
CONSPIRATORIAL	GRUESOME	PORTENTS	VIGOR
DECREED	GUTTURAL	PROFOUND	VULNERABLE
DESECRATE	IMPUDENT	RAUCOUS	
DISCERNIBLE	INDELIBLE	RIVETED	

Devil's Arithmetic Vocabulary Crossword 1

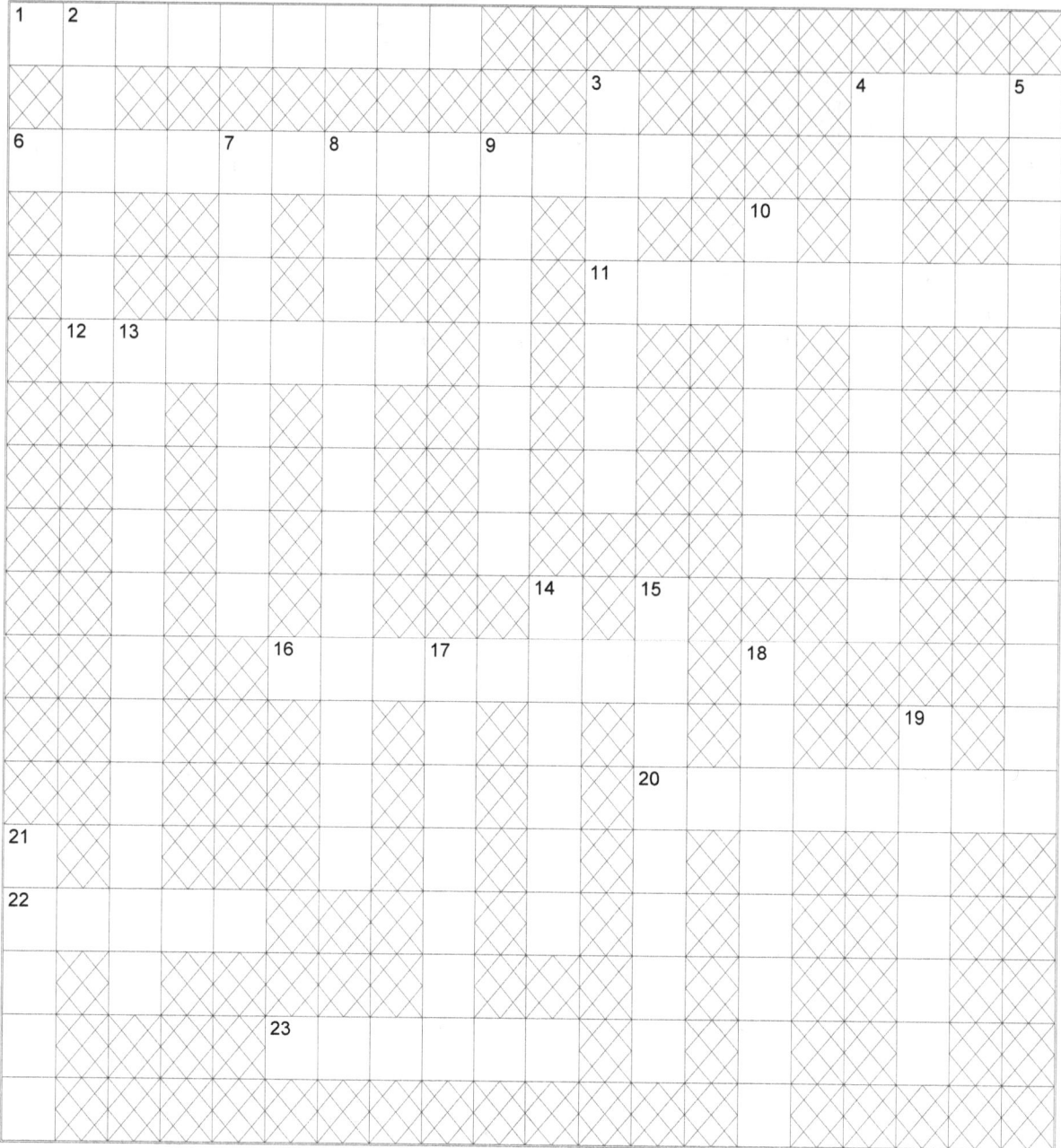

Across
1. Edge; fringe
4. Sour; gloomy
6. Friendly; agreeable
11. Passion; intensity
12. Of Satan
16. Loud, abrupt sounds
20. Shyness
22. Contradiction
23. Skimpy

Down
2. Departure; exit
3. Unclean; untidy
4. Ruin; violate
5. Steadily; constantly
7. Shocked
8. Burning
9. Mixture
10. Heated emotion
13. Approval
14. Tasteless; gaudy
15. Indications; omens
17. Satisfying
18. Bright; shining
19. Position
21. Energy

Devil's Arithmetic Vocabulary Crossword 1 Answer Key

Across
1. Edge; fringe
4. Sour; gloomy
6. Friendly; agreeable
11. Passion; intensity
12. Of Satan
16. Loud, abrupt sounds
20. Shyness
22. Contradiction
23. Skimpy

Down
2. Departure; exit
3. Unclean; untidy
4. Ruin; violate
5. Steadily; constantly
7. Shocked
8. Burning
9. Mixture
10. Heated emotion
13. Approval
14. Tasteless; gaudy
15. Indications; omens
17. Satisfying
18. Bright; shining
19. Position
21. Energy

Devil's Arithmetic Vocabulary Crossword 2

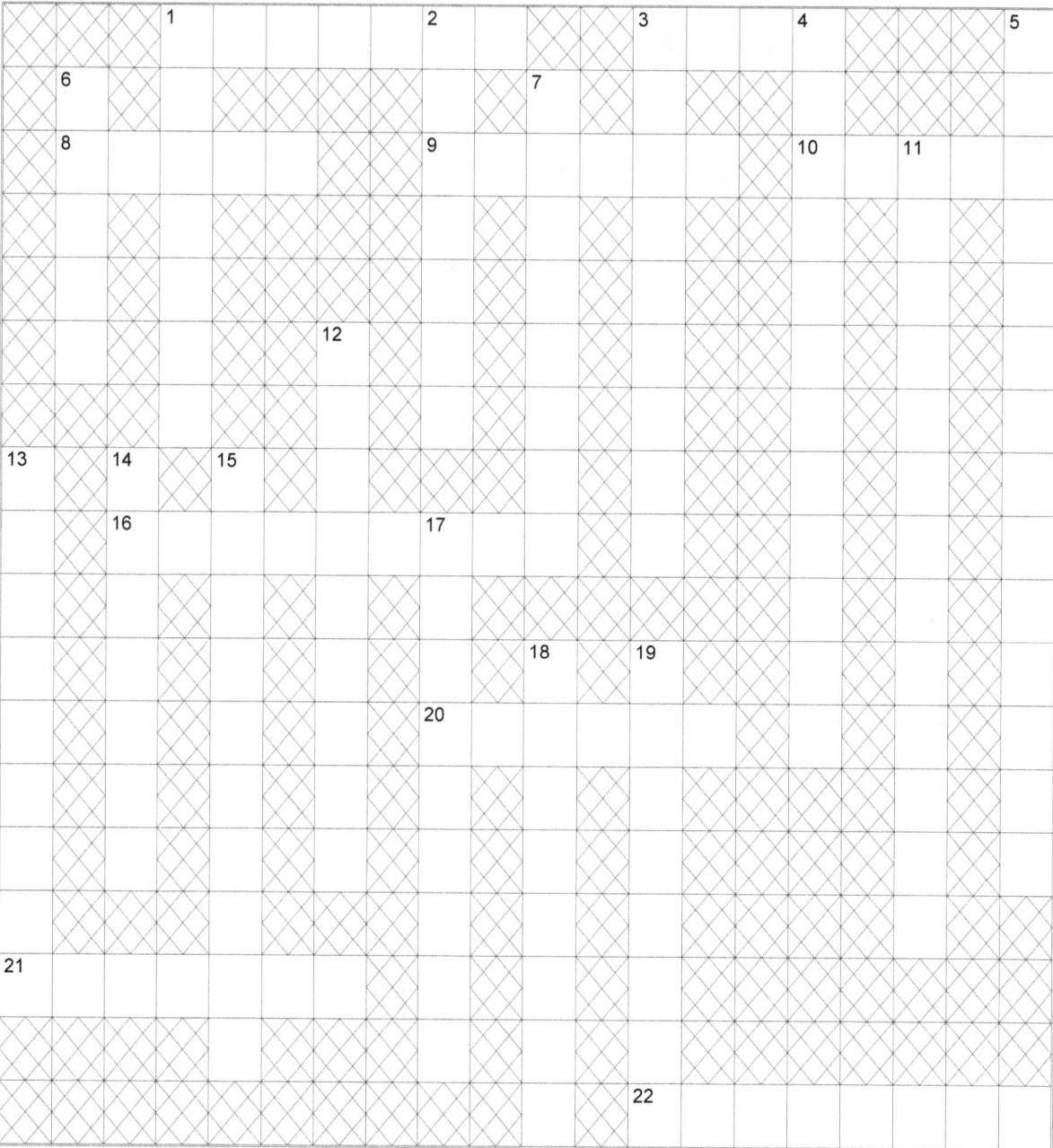

Across
1. Of Satan
3. Sour; gloomy
8. Contradiction
9. Tasteless; gaudy
10. Clear-headed
16. Humiliated
20. Departure; exit
21. Puzzling; slippery
22. Loud, abrupt sounds

Down
1. Unclean; untidy
2. Ungrateful person
3. Ruin; violate
4. Steadily; constantly
5. Unable to solve
6. Energy
7. Heavy; penetrating
11. Friendly; agreeable
12. Edge; fringe
13. Passion; intensity
14. Mixture
15. Furnace used for cremation
17. Permanent; unforgetting
18. Indications; omens
19. Bright; shining

Devil's Arithmetic Vocabulary Crossword 2 Answer Key

		1 S	A	T	A	2 N	I	C		3 D	O	4 U	R		5 U
	6 V		L			N		7 P		E		R			N
	8 I	R	O	N	Y	9 G	A	R	I	S	H	10 L	U	11 C	I	D
	G		V			R		O		E		L		O		E
	O		E			A		F		C		E		M		C
	R		N		12 P	T		O		R		T		P		I
			S		E		E		U		A		L		A		P
13 V		14 A		15 C	R			N		T		E		N		H
E		16 M	O	R	T	I	F	17 I	E	D		E		S		I		E
H		A		E		P		N						S		O		R
E		L		M		H		D		18 P		19 L		L		N		A
M		G		A		E		20 E	X	O	D	U	S		Y		A		B
E		A		T		R		L		R		M				B		L
N		M		O		Y		I		T		I				L		E
C				R				B		E		N				E		
21 E	L	U	S	I	V	E		L		N		O						
				A				E		T		U						
								S		22 S	T	A	C	C	A	T	O

Across
1. Of Satan
3. Sour; gloomy
8. Contradiction
9. Tasteless; gaudy
10. Clear-headed
16. Humiliated
20. Departure; exit
21. Puzzling; slippery
22. Loud, abrupt sounds

Down
1. Unclean; untidy
2. Ungrateful person
3. Ruin; violate
4. Steadily; constantly
5. Unable to solve
6. Energy
7. Heavy; penetrating
11. Friendly; agreeable
12. Edge; fringe
13. Passion; intensity
14. Mixture
15. Furnace used for cremation
17. Permanent; unforgetting
18. Indications; omens
19. Bright; shining

Devil's Arithmetic Vocabulary Crossword 3

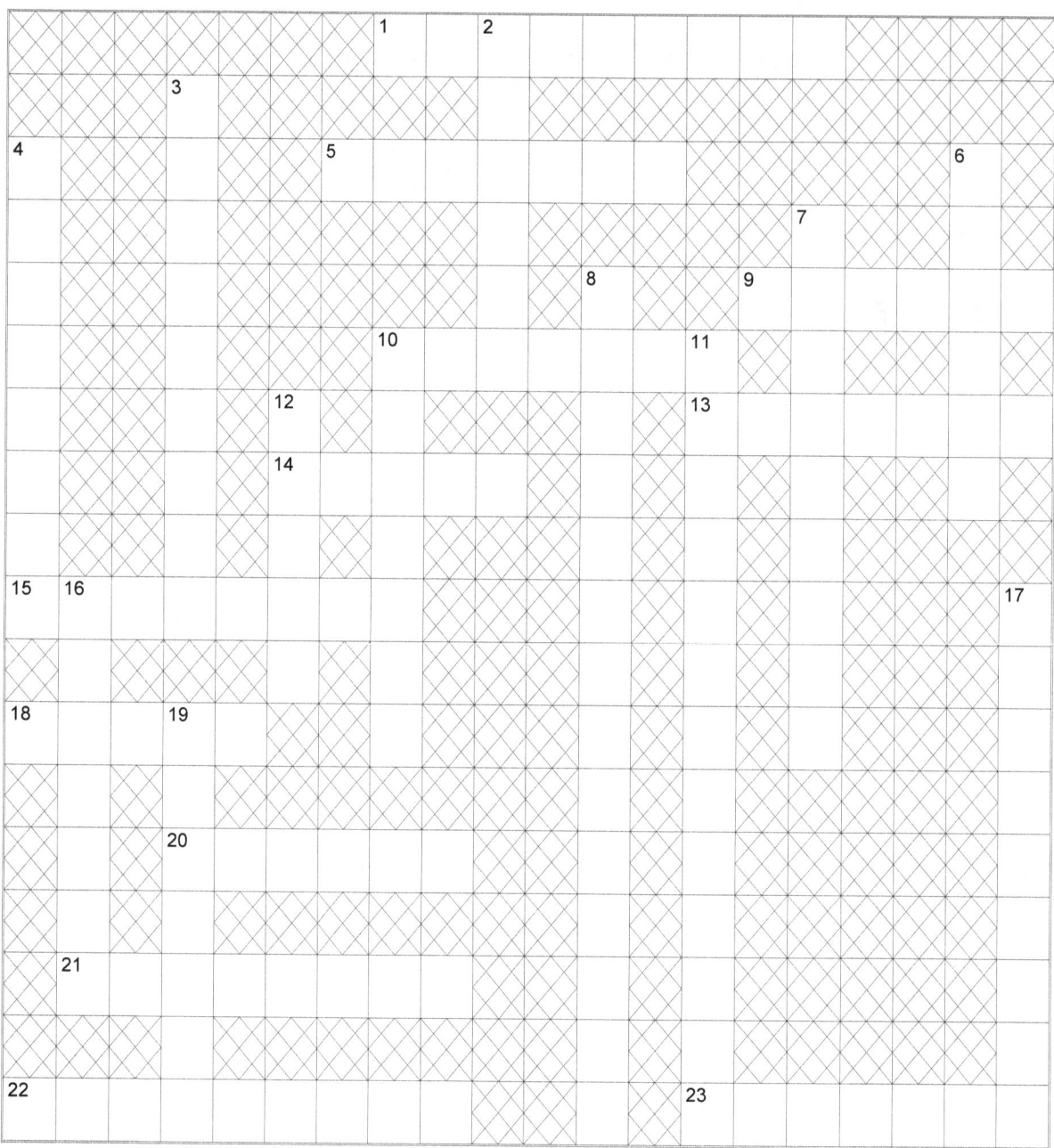

Across
1. Erratic; inconsistent
5. Mixture
9. Heated emotion
10. Of Satan
13. Threatening
14. Contradiction
15. Horrible
18. Clear-headed
20. Tasteless; gaudy
21. Loud, abrupt sounds
22. Passion; intensity
23. Puzzling; slippery

Down
2. Position
3. Ruin; violate
4. Bouncing; bumping
6. Departure; exit
7. Edge; fringe
8. Unable to solve
10. Unclean; untidy
11. Friendly; agreeable
12. Energy
16. Loud; piercing
17. Widespread
19. Ungrateful person

Devil's Arithmetic Vocabulary Crossword 3 Answer Key

Across
1. ARBITRARY
5. AMALGAM
9. FERVOR
10. SATANIC
13. OMINOUS
14. IRONY
15. GRUESOME
18. LUCID
20. GARISH
21. STACCATO
22. VEHEMENCE
23. ELUSIVE

Down
2. IBIS (?)
3. DESECRATE
4. JOSTLING
6. EXODUS
7. PERIPHERY
8. UNDECIPHERABLE
10. SLOVENLY
11. CORDIAL
12. VIGOR
16. RESOUNDING
17. PERVASIVE
19. INGRATE

Clues

Across
1. Erratic; inconsistent
5. Mixture
9. Heated emotion
10. Of Satan
13. Threatening
14. Contradiction
15. Horrible
18. Clear-headed
20. Tasteless; gaudy
21. Loud, abrupt sounds
22. Passion; intensity
23. Puzzling; slippery

Down
2. Position
3. Ruin; violate
4. Bouncing; bumping
6. Departure; exit
7. Edge; fringe
8. Unable to solve
10. Unclean; untidy
11. Friendly; agreeable
12. Energy
16. Loud; piercing
17. Widespread
19. Ungrateful person

Devil's Arithmetic Vocabulary Crossword 4

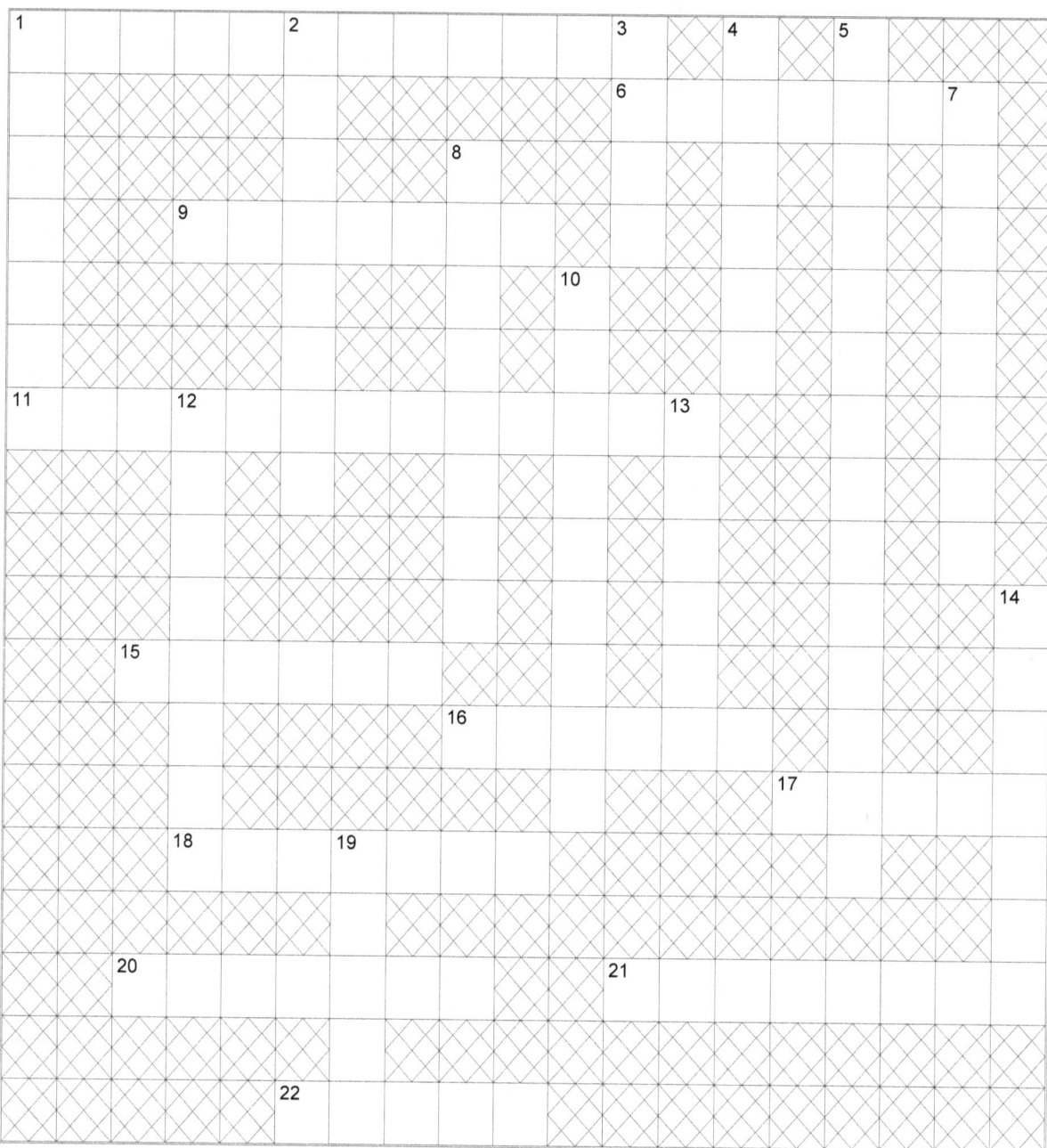

Across
1. One image on top of another
6. Threatening
9. Loud; piercing
11. Friendly; agreeable
15. Heated emotion
16. Tasteless; gaudy
17. Showy
18. Unclean; untidy
20. Mixture
21. Bouncing; bumping
22. Contradiction

Down
1. Of Satan
2. Cocky; arrogant
3. Sour; gloomy
4. Position
5. Secretly plotting
7. Loud, abrupt sounds
8. Bright; shining
10. Erratic; inconsistent
12. Indications; omens
13. Departure; exit
14. Satisfying
19. Energy

Devil's Arithmetic Vocabulary Crossword 4 Answer Key

Across
1. One image on top of another
6. Threatening
9. Loud; piercing
11. Friendly; agreeable
15. Heated emotion
16. Tasteless; gaudy
17. Showy
18. Unclean; untidy
20. Mixture
21. Bouncing; bumping
22. Contradiction

Down
1. Of Satan
2. Cocky; arrogant
3. Sour; gloomy
4. Position
5. Secretly plotting
7. Loud, abrupt sounds
8. Bright; shining
10. Erratic; inconsistent
12. Indications; omens
13. Departure; exit
14. Satisfying
19. Energy

Devil's Arithmetic Vocabulary Juggle Letters 1

1. EREMUOGS = 1. _____
   Horrible

2. IEICBLNERSD = 2. _____
   Recognizable

3. IDTIYITM = 3. _____
   Shyness

4. TPSNTROE = 4. _____
   Indications; omens

5. EOLSNSV = 5. _____
   Unclean; untidy

6. EVSVRPAEI = 6. _____
   Widespread

7. REBNEPHUEICALD = 7. _____
   Unable to solve

8. UOFORDNP = 8. _____
   Heavy; penetrating

9. AAIRYTRBR = 9. _____
   Erratic; inconsistent

10. LCGNOYI = 10. _____
    Satisfying

11. DRVEEIT = 11. _____
    Attention drawn to

12. DTRIDSOTE = 12. _____
    Deformed; twisted

13. ROUD = 13. _____
    Sour; gloomy

14. OARCSUU = 14. _____
    Loud; piercing

15. RGEEMA = 15. _____
    Skimpy

Devil's Arithmetic Vocabulary Juggle Letters 1 Answer Key

1. EREMUOGS = 1. GRUESOME
   Horrible

2. IEICBLNERSD = 2. DISCERNIBLE
   Recognizable

3. IDTIYITM = 3. TIMIDITY
   Shyness

4. TPSNTROE = 4. PORTENTS
   Indications; omens

5. EOLSNSV = 5. SLOVENS
   Unclean; untidy

6. EVSVRPAEI = 6. PERVASIVE
   Widespread

7. REBNEPHUEICALD = 7. UNDECIPHERABLE
   Unable to solve

8. UOFORDNP = 8. PROFOUND
   Heavy; penetrating

9. AAIRYTRBR = 9. ARBITRARY
   Erratic; inconsistent

10. LCGNOYI =10. CLOYING
    Satisfying

11. DRVEEIT =11. RIVETED
    Attention drawn to

12. DTRIDSOTE =12. DISTORTED
    Deformed; twisted

13. ROUD =13. DOUR
    Sour; gloomy

14. OARCSUU =14. RAUCOUS
    Loud; piercing

15. RGEEMA =15. MEAGER
    Skimpy

Devil's Arithmetic Vocabulary Juggle Letters 2

1. ROINY = 1. _____
   Contradiction

2. SOUOINM = 2. _____
   Threatening

3. STPRNOET = 3. _____
   Indications; omens

4. SIOSCEOMRNP = 4. _____
   Reduction

5. LBENEIILD = 5. _____
   Permanent; unforgetting

6. OARTMICREA = 6. _____
   Furnace used for cremation

7. OVRRFE = 7. _____
   Heated emotion

8. IUUMSNLO = 8. _____
   Bright; shining

9. LNLVUARBEE = 9. _____
   Defenseless; exposed

10. OLESVSN =10. _____
    Unclean; untidy

11. HEPRREIPY =11. _____
    Edge; fringe

12. NINUHIEDBASGTIUSL =12. _____
    Unable to distinguish

13. OESUDX =13. _____
    Departure; exit

14. AUEENLNDEV =14. _____
    Made without yeast

15. UEDHMNIZEDA =15. _____
    Deprived of human dignity

106
Copyrighted

Devil's Arithmetic Vocabulary Juggle Letters 2 Answer Key

1. ROINY = 1. IRONY
Contradiction

2. SOUOINM = 2. OMINOUS
Threatening

3. STPRNOET = 3. PORTENTS
Indications; omens

4. SIOSCEOMRNP = 4. COMPRESSION
Reduction

5. LBENEIILD = 5. INDELIBLE
Permanent; unforgetting

6. OARTMICREA = 6. CREMATORIA
Furnace used for cremation

7. OVRRFE = 7. FERVOR
Heated emotion

8. IUUMSNLO = 8. LUMINOUS
Bright; shining

9. LNLVUARBEE = 9. VULNERABLE
Defenseless; exposed

10. OLESVSN = 10. SLOVENS
Unclean; untidy

11. HEPRREIPY = 11. PERIPHERY
Edge; fringe

12. NINUHIEDBASGTIUSL = 12. UNDISTINGUISHABLE
Unable to distinguish

13. OESUDX = 13. EXODUS
Departure; exit

14. AUEENLNDEV = 14. UNLEAVENED
Made without yeast

15. UEDHMNIZEDA = 15. DEHUMANIZED
Deprived of human dignity

Devil's Arithmetic Vocabulary Juggle Letters 3

1. EEMZERIMDS = 1. _____
   Hypnotized; captivated

2. VRRFOE = 2. _____
   Heated emotion

3. MESOTNCANPIO = 3. _____
   Benefits

4. MISESNORCPO = 4. _____
   Reduction

5. IEPLONAANCBOM = 5. _____
   Friendly; agreeable

6. EVSEULI = 6. _____
   Puzzling; slippery

7. NRTAEGI = 7. _____
   Ungrateful person

8. SETRENSLELLY = 8. _____
   Steadily; constantly

9. AGERME = 9. _____
   Skimpy

10. IONCLYG =10. _____
    Satisfying

11. OSLNJTIG =11. _____
    Bouncing; bumping

12. TIPUDNEM =12. _____
    Cocky; arrogant

13. IDGITPNSAIS =13. _____
    Disappearing

14. URBEIHDNS =14. _____
    Polished; waxed

15. RCNANIIOEINT =15. _____
    Burning

Devil's Arithmetic Vocabulary Juggle Letters 3 Answer Key

1. EEMZERIMDS = 1. MESMERIZED
Hypnotized; captivated

2. VRRFOE = 2. FERVOR
Heated emotion

3. MESOTNCANPIO = 3. COMPENSATION
Benefits

4. MISESNORCPO = 4. COMPRESSION
Reduction

5. IEPLONAANCBOM = 5. COMPANIONABLE
Friendly; agreeable

6. EVSEULI = 6. ELUSIVE
Puzzling; slippery

7. NRTAEGI = 7. INGRATE
Ungrateful person

8. SETRENSLELLY = 8. RELENTLESSLY
Steadily; constantly

9. AGERME = 9. MEAGER
Skimpy

10. IONCLYG =10. CLOYING
Satisfying

11. OSLNJTIG =11. JOSTLING
Bouncing; bumping

12. TIPUDNEM =12. IMPUDENT
Cocky; arrogant

13. IDGITPNSAIS =13. DISSIPATING
Disappearing

14. URBEIHDNS =14. BURNISHED
Polished; waxed

15. RCNANIIOEINT =15. INCINERATION
Burning

Devil's Arithmetic Vocabulary Juggle Letters 4

1. NSSOEVL = 1. _____
   Unclean; untidy

2. SYELERLTNESL = 2. _____
   Steadily; constantly

3. UGESUIHLNTANIDSBI = 3. _____
   Unable to distinguish

4. YUAGD = 4. _____
   Showy

5. IIORTMEDF = 5. _____
   Humiliated

6. RSMEUEOG = 6. _____
   Horrible

7. DAALENEIT = 7. _____
   Distances

8. OSNOOSUR = 8. _____
   Deep; full sounded

9. EONDPINMUGNYRCEHL = 9. _____
   Without understanding

10. ALGMMAA = 10. _____
    Mixture

11. ARTIAECMOR = 11. _____
    Furnace used for cremation

12. IZUOIRTANOITN = 12. _____
    Put into a system

13. OEPTSIMAONCN = 13. _____
    Benefits

14. RATYRAIRB = 14. _____
    Erratic; inconsistent

15. ORYIN = 15. _____
    Contradiction

Devil's Arithmetic Vocabulary Juggle Letters 4 Answer Key

1. NSSOEVL = 1. SLOVENS
Unclean; untidy

2. SYELERLTNESL = 2. RELENTLESSLY
Steadily; constantly

3. UGESUIHLNTANIDSBI = 3. UNDISTINGUISHABLE
Unable to distinguish

4. YUAGD = 4. GAUDY
Showy

5. IIORTMEDF = 5. MORTIFIED
Humiliated

6. RSMEUEOG = 6. GRUESOME
Horrible

7. DAALENEIT = 7. ALIENATED
Distances

8. OSNOOSUR = 8. SONOROUS
Deep; full sounded

9. EONDPINMUGNYRCEHL = 9. UNCOMPREHENDINGLY
Without understanding

10. ALGMMAA = 10. AMALGAM
Mixture

11. ARTIAECMOR = 11. CREMATORIA
Furnace used for cremation

12. IZUOIRTANOITN = 12. ROUTINIZATION
Put into a system

13. OEPTSIMAONCN = 13. COMPENSATION
Benefits

14. RATYRAIRB = 14. ARBITRARY
Erratic; inconsistent

15. ORYIN = 15. IRONY
Contradiction

AFFIRMATION	Approval
ALIENATED	Distances
AMALGAM	Mixture
APPALLED	Shocked
ARBITRARY	Erratic; inconsistent
BILLET	Position

BURNISHED	Polished; waxed
CLOYING	Satisfying
COMPANIONABLE	Friendly; agreeable
COMPENSATION	Benefits
COMPRESSION	Reduction
CONSPIRATORIAL	Secretly plotting

CREMATORIA	Furnace used for cremation
DECREED	Ordered
DEHUMANIZED	Deprived of human dignity
DESECRATE	Ruin; violate
DISCERNIBLE	Recognizable
DISSIPATING	Disappearing

DISTORTED	Deformed; twisted
DOUR	Sour; gloomy
ELUSIVE	Puzzling; slippery
EXODUS	Departure; exit
FERVOR	Heated emotion
GARISH	Tasteless; gaudy

GAUDY	Showy
GRUESOME	Horrible
GUTTURAL	Throaty; gravelly
IMPUDENT	Cocky; arrogant
INCINERATION	Burning
INDELIBLE	Permanent; unforgetting

INGRATE	Ungrateful person
IRONY	Contradiction
JOSTLING	Bouncing; bumping
LUCID	Clear-headed
LUMINOUS	Bright; shining
MEAGER	Skimpy

MESMERIZED	Hypnotized; captivated
MORTIFIED	Humiliated
OMINOUS	Threatening
PERIPHERY	Edge; fringe
PERVASIVE	Widespread
PORTENTS	Indications; omens

PROFOUND	Heavy; penetrating
RAUCOUS	Loud; piercing
RELENTLESSLY	Steadily; constantly
RIVETED	Attention drawn to
ROUTINIZATION	Put into a system
SATANIC	Of Satan

SLOVENS	Unclean; untidy
SONOROUS	Deep; full sounded
STACCATO	Loud, abrupt sounds
SUPERIMPOSED	One image on top of another
TIMIDITY	Shyness
UNCOMPREHENDINGLY	Without understanding

UNDECIPHERABLE	Unable to solve
UNDISTINGUISHABLE	Unable to distinguish
UNLEAVENED	Made without yeast
VEHEMENCE	Passion; intensity
VIGOR	Energy
VULNERABLE	Defenseless; exposed

Devil's Arithmetic Vocabulary

DISTORTED	OMINOUS	PERVASIVE	UNLEAVENED	AFFIRMATION
GAUDY	DESECRATE	VEHEMENCE	SUPERIMPOSED	GUTTURAL
IRONY	CREMATORIA	FREE SPACE	EXODUS	ALIENATED
PORTENTS	ELUSIVE	APPALLED	ARBITRARY	UNDECIPHERABLE
DEHUMANIZED	SLOVENS	JOSTLING	GRUESOME	COMPENSATION

Devil's Arithmetic Vocabulary

PROFOUND	UNDISTINGUISHABLE	MEAGER	AMALGAM	INDELIBLE
INCINERATION	CLOYING	RAUCOUS	RELENTLESSLY	TIMIDITY
BILLET	DISSIPATING	FREE SPACE	PERIPHERY	LUCID
SATANIC	INGRATE	MORTIFIED	DISCERNIBLE	UNCOMPREHENDINGLY
VULNERABLE	DOUR	ROUTINIZATION	SONOROUS	RIVETED

Devil's Arithmetic Vocabulary

GARISH	CLOYING	PROFOUND	STACCATO	INGRATE
COMPENSATION	TIMIDITY	RIVETED	LUMINOUS	BILLET
GRUESOME	RAUCOUS	FREE SPACE	MORTIFIED	ELUSIVE
ARBITRARY	LUCID	IRONY	ALIENATED	ROUTINIZATION
DECREED	UNLEAVENED	SLOVENS	INDELIBLE	OMINOUS

Devil's Arithmetic Vocabulary

COMPRESSION	RELENTLESSLY	CONSPIRATORIAL	FERVOR	VEHEMENCE
SUPERIMPOSED	GAUDY	UNDECIPHERABLE	JOSTLING	UNCOMPREHENDINGLY
BURNISHED	DISTORTED	FREE SPACE	IMPUDENT	PORTENTS
INCINERATION	DEHUMANIZED	PERIPHERY	MEAGER	AMALGAM
SONOROUS	DESECRATE	UNDISTINGUISHABLE	AFFIRMATION	CREMATORIA

Devil's Arithmetic Vocabulary

RELENTLESSLY	LUMINOUS	GARISH	UNDECIPHERABLE	MEAGER
STACCATO	COMPENSATION	DESECRATE	INCINERATION	OMINOUS
UNLEAVENED	ALIENATED	FREE SPACE	CREMATORIA	SATANIC
UNDISTINGUISHABLE	IMPUDENT	AFFIRMATION	MESMERIZED	GAUDY
PORTENTS	GRUESOME	SLOVENS	CONSPIRATORIAL	APPALLED

Devil's Arithmetic Vocabulary

FERVOR	RAUCOUS	IRONY	INGRATE	VEHEMENCE
VIGOR	GUTTURAL	LUCID	TIMIDITY	DISSIPATING
MORTIFIED	DEHUMANIZED	FREE SPACE	PROFOUND	DOUR
SONOROUS	INDELIBLE	BURNISHED	ARBITRARY	DISCERNIBLE
UNCOMPREHENDINGLY	DISTORTED	COMPRESSION	SUPERIMPOSED	BILLET

Devil's Arithmetic Vocabulary

RIVETED	RELENTLESSLY	RAUCOUS	GARISH	DISSIPATING
DOUR	ALIENATED	BURNISHED	CLOYING	MORTIFIED
OMINOUS	PERVASIVE	FREE SPACE	DISCERNIBLE	COMPENSATION
INDELIBLE	SONOROUS	ELUSIVE	DEHUMANIZED	INCINERATION
DESECRATE	PERIPHERY	BILLET	EXODUS	SUPERIMPOSED

Devil's Arithmetic Vocabulary

COMPRESSION	STACCATO	SLOVENS	DECREED	ARBITRARY
PORTENTS	PROFOUND	DISTORTED	JOSTLING	FERVOR
VULNERABLE	MESMERIZED	FREE SPACE	CONSPIRATORIAL	TIMIDITY
APPALLED	UNDISTINGUISHABLE	ROUTINIZATION	COMPANIONABLE	AMALGAM
CREMATORIA	UNLEAVENED	VIGOR	LUMINOUS	UNDECIPHERABLE

Devil's Arithmetic Vocabulary

MORTIFIED	EXODUS	BILLET	STACCATO	DECREED
SLOVENS	VIGOR	DISSIPATING	PROFOUND	LUMINOUS
SUPERIMPOSED	PORTENTS	FREE SPACE	DOUR	CONSPIRATORIAL
RIVETED	ROUTINIZATION	MESMERIZED	BURNISHED	GAUDY
INCINERATION	AFFIRMATION	AMALGAM	APPALLED	DESECRATE

Devil's Arithmetic Vocabulary

IRONY	CREMATORIA	SATANIC	DISTORTED	SONOROUS
PERIPHERY	FERVOR	INGRATE	ARBITRARY	COMPENSATION
UNLEAVENED	CLOYING	FREE SPACE	MEAGER	GUTTURAL
UNDISTINGUISHABLE	ELUSIVE	UNDECIPHERABLE	COMPANIONABLE	RAUCOUS
UNCOMPREHENDINGLY	ALIENATED	GRUESOME	TIMIDITY	DEHUMANIZED

Devil's Arithmetic Vocabulary

VIGOR	IMPUDENT	MESMERIZED	SONOROUS	CLOYING
CREMATORIA	AMALGAM	GRUESOME	TIMIDITY	RAUCOUS
APPALLED	MORTIFIED	FREE SPACE	GUTTURAL	ROUTINIZATION
CONSPIRATORIAL	DECREED	IRONY	DOUR	INCINERATION
COMPENSATION	SLOVENS	OMINOUS	UNDISTINGUISHABLE	VULNERABLE

Devil's Arithmetic Vocabulary

RELENTLESSLY	INGRATE	EXODUS	DESECRATE	VEHEMENCE
MEAGER	RIVETED	DISCERNIBLE	ALIENATED	DEHUMANIZED
DISTORTED	BURNISHED	FREE SPACE	SATANIC	GARISH
ARBITRARY	ELUSIVE	UNLEAVENED	PERVASIVE	INDELIBLE
JOSTLING	PERIPHERY	LUMINOUS	PORTENTS	PROFOUND

Devil's Arithmetic Vocabulary

LUCID	AFFIRMATION	GAUDY	COMPENSATION	UNDISTINGUISHABLE
STACCATO	GRUESOME	DECREED	RIVETED	SUPERIMPOSED
ROUTINIZATION	DEHUMANIZED	FREE SPACE	INCINERATION	CLOYING
COMPRESSION	AMALGAM	RELENTLESSLY	VEHEMENCE	DESECRATE
APPALLED	UNCOMPREHENDINGLY	SONOROUS	UNLEAVENED	MEAGER

Devil's Arithmetic Vocabulary

DISSIPATING	DOUR	IMPUDENT	PROFOUND	FERVOR
ELUSIVE	BURNISHED	ALIENATED	MESMERIZED	VULNERABLE
IRONY	PORTENTS	FREE SPACE	DISCERNIBLE	ARBITRARY
CREMATORIA	BILLET	RAUCOUS	LUMINOUS	SLOVENS
MORTIFIED	OMINOUS	INGRATE	GUTTURAL	PERIPHERY

Devil's Arithmetic Vocabulary

VIGOR	RELENTLESSLY	PROFOUND	ARBITRARY	DISSIPATING
TIMIDITY	INCINERATION	UNDECIPHERABLE	IMPUDENT	BILLET
BURNISHED	AFFIRMATION	FREE SPACE	SONOROUS	IRONY
PERIPHERY	MORTIFIED	DEHUMANIZED	VEHEMENCE	RAUCOUS
FERVOR	COMPANIONABLE	INGRATE	RIVETED	CREMATORIA

Devil's Arithmetic Vocabulary

JOSTLING	SLOVENS	AMALGAM	GAUDY	GRUESOME
APPALLED	COMPENSATION	ALIENATED	DISTORTED	ROUTINIZATION
INDELIBLE	COMPRESSION	FREE SPACE	LUMINOUS	DECREED
SUPERIMPOSED	DISCERNIBLE	STACCATO	OMINOUS	MESMERIZED
CONSPIRATORIAL	GUTTURAL	EXODUS	GARISH	DOUR

Devil's Arithmetic Vocabulary

RELENTLESSLY	PERIPHERY	DECREED	JOSTLING	DISCERNIBLE
IRONY	SONOROUS	COMPANIONABLE	DISTORTED	GARISH
MORTIFIED	VIGOR	FREE SPACE	ROUTINIZATION	COMPENSATION
MEAGER	SLOVENS	UNDECIPHERABLE	UNDISTINGUISHABLE	SUPERIMPOSED
RIVETED	INCINERATION	IMPUDENT	MESMERIZED	BILLET

Devil's Arithmetic Vocabulary

AMALGAM	TIMIDITY	CREMATORIA	VEHEMENCE	COMPRESSION
DESECRATE	DOUR	DISSIPATING	PERVASIVE	PROFOUND
PORTENTS	UNCOMPREHENDINGLY	FREE SPACE	VULNERABLE	ARBITRARY
STACCATO	AFFIRMATION	FERVOR	CONSPIRATORIAL	GRUESOME
ALIENATED	GAUDY	UNLEAVENED	EXODUS	CLOYING

Devil's Arithmetic Vocabulary

DECREED	DOUR	DISCERNIBLE	ELUSIVE	BURNISHED
RAUCOUS	EXODUS	IRONY	RIVETED	VEHEMENCE
ARBITRARY	UNDECIPHERABLE	FREE SPACE	SONOROUS	STACCATO
DISSIPATING	AFFIRMATION	COMPANIONABLE	CONSPIRATORIAL	GARISH
COMPENSATION	PORTENTS	RELENTLESSLY	LUMINOUS	VIGOR

Devil's Arithmetic Vocabulary

SATANIC	UNCOMPREHENDINGLY	MESMERIZED	APPALLED	MORTIFIED
ALIENATED	AMALGAM	COMPRESSION	CLOYING	DEHUMANIZED
PROFOUND	TIMIDITY	FREE SPACE	GRUESOME	GUTTURAL
DISTORTED	INGRATE	SLOVENS	UNDISTINGUISHABLE	OMINOUS
INCINERATION	UNLEAVENED	JOSTLING	INDELIBLE	GAUDY

Devil's Arithmetic Vocabulary

VEHEMENCE	PERIPHERY	OMINOUS	CREMATORIA	BILLET
LUMINOUS	GAUDY	ALIENATED	DISSIPATING	ARBITRARY
STACCATO	RELENTLESSLY	FREE SPACE	DISTORTED	GUTTURAL
RAUCOUS	CLOYING	UNLEAVENED	SUPERIMPOSED	EXODUS
DEHUMANIZED	DISCERNIBLE	DOUR	INCINERATION	CONSPIRATORIAL

Devil's Arithmetic Vocabulary

UNDISTINGUISHABLE	COMPENSATION	COMPRESSION	IRONY	MESMERIZED
GRUESOME	LUCID	VIGOR	IMPUDENT	MEAGER
APPALLED	INDELIBLE	FREE SPACE	SATANIC	JOSTLING
PROFOUND	BURNISHED	UNDECIPHERABLE	UNCOMPREHENDINGLY	AMALGAM
GARISH	SONOROUS	FERVOR	RIVETED	VULNERABLE

Devil's Arithmetic Vocabulary

OMINOUS	FERVOR	ALIENATED	GRUESOME	ROUTINIZATION
SONOROUS	PROFOUND	AMALGAM	INCINERATION	DECREED
COMPRESSION	UNCOMPREHENDINGLY	FREE SPACE	RAUCOUS	ELUSIVE
MEAGER	PERIPHERY	IRONY	UNDECIPHERABLE	GAUDY
CREMATORIA	SUPERIMPOSED	UNDISTINGUISHABLE	RIVETED	JOSTLING

Devil's Arithmetic Vocabulary

DOUR	GUTTURAL	INGRATE	TIMIDITY	INDELIBLE
PORTENTS	UNLEAVENED	IMPUDENT	ARBITRARY	BILLET
MORTIFIED	COMPANIONABLE	FREE SPACE	COMPENSATION	DESECRATE
VEHEMENCE	DISCERNIBLE	STACCATO	BURNISHED	MESMERIZED
VIGOR	AFFIRMATION	DISSIPATING	SLOVENS	VULNERABLE

Devil's Arithmetic Vocabulary

TIMIDITY	SUPERIMPOSED	CONSPIRATORIAL	PERVASIVE	AMALGAM
LUMINOUS	RAUCOUS	AFFIRMATION	RIVETED	ELUSIVE
SLOVENS	BILLET	FREE SPACE	ALIENATED	VEHEMENCE
OMINOUS	DISTORTED	GAUDY	INGRATE	PROFOUND
EXODUS	DEHUMANIZED	MESMERIZED	GRUESOME	ARBITRARY

Devil's Arithmetic Vocabulary

INCINERATION	APPALLED	PORTENTS	GARISH	IMPUDENT
BURNISHED	LUCID	STACCATO	DECREED	PERIPHERY
JOSTLING	SATANIC	FREE SPACE	COMPENSATION	FERVOR
DESECRATE	ROUTINIZATION	COMPANIONABLE	UNDISTINGUISHABLE	RELENTLESSLY
CREMATORIA	COMPRESSION	UNCOMPREHENDINGLY	DISSIPATING	GUTTURAL

Devil's Arithmetic Vocabulary

CLOYING	ARBITRARY	PROFOUND	EXODUS	STACCATO
PERVASIVE	IRONY	VULNERABLE	MEAGER	DEHUMANIZED
INDELIBLE	VEHEMENCE	FREE SPACE	UNDECIPHERABLE	APPALLED
BURNISHED	OMINOUS	SATANIC	UNCOMPREHENDINGLY	RAUCOUS
MESMERIZED	BILLET	DISSIPATING	GRUESOME	TIMIDITY

Devil's Arithmetic Vocabulary

COMPANIONABLE	COMPRESSION	UNLEAVENED	AFFIRMATION	RELENTLESSLY
GUTTURAL	RIVETED	SONOROUS	DESECRATE	CREMATORIA
ROUTINIZATION	GARISH	FREE SPACE	LUCID	PORTENTS
SUPERIMPOSED	FERVOR	INGRATE	CONSPIRATORIAL	DISTORTED
DISCERNIBLE	DOUR	LUMINOUS	INCINERATION	ELUSIVE

Devil's Arithmetic Vocabulary

VEHEMENCE	BURNISHED	MORTIFIED	ARBITRARY	CREMATORIA
COMPENSATION	UNDECIPHERABLE	COMPRESSION	LUMINOUS	AFFIRMATION
PORTENTS	INDELIBLE	FREE SPACE	VULNERABLE	CLOYING
DECREED	RELENTLESSLY	GARISH	TIMIDITY	IRONY
GRUESOME	COMPANIONABLE	SLOVENS	JOSTLING	GAUDY

Devil's Arithmetic Vocabulary

PROFOUND	BILLET	MEAGER	SATANIC	IMPUDENT
VIGOR	DISSIPATING	UNLEAVENED	LUCID	DISCERNIBLE
AMALGAM	GUTTURAL	FREE SPACE	DEHUMANIZED	OMINOUS
MESMERIZED	DISTORTED	APPALLED	DESECRATE	SONOROUS
ALIENATED	EXODUS	RIVETED	RAUCOUS	FERVOR

Copyrighted

Devil's Arithmetic Vocabulary

LUMINOUS	PROFOUND	DISSIPATING	RAUCOUS	DESECRATE
GUTTURAL	UNDECIPHERABLE	VEHEMENCE	UNLEAVENED	MEAGER
COMPRESSION	DISTORTED	FREE SPACE	DEHUMANIZED	JOSTLING
DISCERNIBLE	UNCOMPREHENDINGLY	OMINOUS	INGRATE	LUCID
UNDISTINGUISHABLE	DECREED	MORTIFIED	PERIPHERY	RIVETED

Devil's Arithmetic Vocabulary

SUPERIMPOSED	AFFIRMATION	EXODUS	APPALLED	GAUDY
GRUESOME	VIGOR	ROUTINIZATION	FERVOR	VULNERABLE
PERVASIVE	INCINERATION	FREE SPACE	ALIENATED	PORTENTS
IRONY	ARBITRARY	ELUSIVE	CREMATORIA	MESMERIZED
DOUR	CLOYING	AMALGAM	STACCATO	CONSPIRATORIAL

www.ingramcontent.com/pod-product-compliance
Lightning Source LLC
Chambersburg PA
CBHW081455070526
44586CB00019B/2358